INFORMATION and COMMUNICATION TECHNOLOGY

for GCSE

COURSEWORK BOOK

Brian Sargent

Contents

Introduction

In the OCR GCSE ICT A specification, coursework makes up 60% of your final mark. All the help given in this book is for the OCR syllabus A for GCSE ICT.

There are two courses, the full course and the short course. For the short course you have to complete two pieces of work: Project 1A and Project 1B. For the full course you have to do another project: Project 2 (help on this piece of coursework is given in chapter 6). The marks available for the three different pieces of coursework are:

- Project 1a : 28 marks
- Project 1b : 28 marks
- Project 2 : 56 marks.

The marks for Project 1a and 1b are added together to give a total of 56 marks. Up to 4 extra marks are then given for how clearly you have written up your work, giving a mark out of 60. These extra 4 marks are also given for Project 2.

Section A Projects 1a and 1b

For Project 1a you have to show your skills at one of:

- word processing,
- desktop publishing,
- creating a web-site,
- creating a multimedia presentation.

You must collect information from newspapers, magazines and books. You will need to collect pictures from clipart. You will have to search the Internet or search an encyclopaedia on a CD-ROM. As well as being used for your GCSE ICT coursework, this piece of work can be used to help you get your key skills certificate in IT.

For Project 1b you will have to produce a piece of work for which you will have to choose a piece of software from:

- database software,
- modelling software (usually a spreadsheet),
- measuring software, or
- control software.

In both Project 1a and Project 1b the 28 marks are divided up into a number of mark ranges. Each mark range has a number of things you must do. When you have done all of them (you are not allowed to miss even one!) you will get a mark in that range. The number of things you have to do gets bigger the more marks you want to get.

How to plan your work

The illustration on the following page shows an example of a coursework planner. The actual dates have not been included since most schools and teachers work to different deadlines. You have to fill in the actual dates yourself if you were using a planner like this. This example is based on the data-handling (database) strand for Project 1b. At the moment, it is not important for you to understand what you have to do for this piece of coursework. It will be explained later. Remember this is just a guide and you will need to set out your own planner to suit yourself.

Coursework requirements

Things to remember when making your planner:

Your teacher will give you a date when you must hand in your work. Try to finish it one week before your teacher has asked you to hand it in. This will give you a little time to go back and check that you are happy with everything. It also gives you some time in case anything goes wrong.

- Make a separate planner for each project you do.

- Set sensible targets for yourself. The planner included here shows what you have to do to get a Grade B for your coursework.

- Always talk to your teacher first, before starting your plan of work. S/he will know what you can do and can help you to set your targets.

Academic Year 2003/2004

- ICT coursework planner

Date	Syllabus requirement	What I have to do
Week 1 Lesson 1	Identify the required output for a given task;	• Write down the task. Write down what I will use the database for. Write down some of the questions the database will be used to answer.
Week 1 Lesson 2	Construct a method of collecting data based on this output;	Use the list of questions I wrote down last week to make a list of the fields which will go in the database. Draw a data capture form with these fields on (perhaps use a spreadsheet).
Week 2 Lesson 1	Collect a range of data;	Collect cuttings from magazines, newspapers or catalogues. (If the database is a cars database, collect the data from a real car showroom).
Week 2 Lesson 2	Create a database using selected pieces of this data;	To create your database will probably take two or three weeks. Create the database structure. Make sure the fields are the right type and size. Use the data capture form to check that the fields will be long enough.
Week 3 Lesson 1		Type in the data Not every field on the data capture form will have data in it for every record. (If it's a cars database and the data has come from newspapers etc. some information could be missing). Write down the names of the fields which have had to be left out.
Week 3 Lesson 2		If there is more than one newspaper, magazine, catalogue etc. some records may be on the data capture form twice. Remember not to type them in twice.
Week 4 Lesson 1	Visually check the database for accuracy;	Read through the database and see if there are any mistakes. Check it against the data capture form. If there are no errors, put some in. Print the database out and use a highlighter to show the mistakes.
Week 4 Lesson 2	Check the database for accuracy using validation routines;	Make sure you have done some validation checks. If you have not, do some searches on the database. Search for numbers or prices which are not within the range you want. You could search for invalid characters in any y/n fields.
Week 5 Lesson 1	Edit the database in light of the mistakes found.	Correct any data errors in the database. Print out the corrected version.
Week 5 Lesson 2	using more than one condition, search the database for answers to specific questions.	Answer the questions which you listed on Week 1 Lesson 1. Make sure that AND and OR conditions are used in the searches and that they are used at least twice.
Week 6 Lesson 1		Finish off everything

Project 1a has two sets of marks. The main set of marks is based on you producing a piece of work and for this you can get up to 21 marks. There are 7 other marks for 'Additional Skills'.

To make it easier for you, the following advice is based on you producing one piece of work to meet both sets of marks. You will need to write about how you produced it and this will allow you to gain both sets of marks.

For project 1a the piece of work can be any one of the following:

- a document which has been produced using a word-processor;
- a document which has been produced using a desktop publishing package;
- a series of slides using presentation software;
- a series of web pages.

The work you produce must be based on a task you have been set by your teacher or one you have thought up yourself. You are not allowed to do a number of different tasks which are set up simply to get marks for each mark range.

Before you make up your mind about which task you are going to choose you need to make sure which mark ranges you are hoping to reach.

To get marks of 11 or above you will need to produce a **significant** piece of work. This should be at least eight A5 or A4 pages of a document or eight slides in a presentation. Any less than this will mean that you can only gain 10 marks or less.

Suggestions for project 1a tasks

1 Produce a short, illustrated children's book.

Your work should include:
- a suitable cover;
- an advert for the writer on the back cover;
- a simple story in a suitable easy to read font;
- illustrations, which could be clip art.

2 Produce a programme for a school performance.

Your work should include:
- photographs of scenes from the production;
- a list of performers;
- timings of performances;
- details of the performance;
- admission prices to various parts of the theatre/hall.

3 Create a web site to advertise your school.

Your work should include:
- text which tells visitors about the school;
- photographs of the school;
- music made by the school orchestra;
- links to other pages.

4 Produce the advertising material for a car showroom.

Your work should include:
- a brochure describing the main features of the cars being sold – make, model, age, engine size, etc.;
- this brochure should show pictures of the cars on sale;
- a list of prices of the cars.

5 Create a presentation, using a computer, on a topic of your choice.

Your work should include:
- animated text;
- pictures where appropriate;
- suitable video;
- running headers and footers;
- a presentation to an audience;
- a guide to how the presentation was created.

Purpose

Remember that in order to get a mark of more than 4 it is essential when choosing one of the above tasks that you are aware of the **purpose** of it. To gain a reasonable mark there must be a **reason** for producing the end product. If you do not write about a purpose or an audience the highest mark you can get is 4 out of 21.

How to get started

The guidance given here is about the car showroom task. You must use this as guidance to give you ideas and not just copy it out. That could lose you a lot of marks.

Setting out your work

You need to make your work easy for your teacher to mark and easy for the moderator to read. You will need to write up everything you have done. A good idea is to set out your work in different sections. The headings of each section are as follows:

- **Introduction:** In this section you will need to write a paragraph explaining why the car showroom needs advertising.

- **Information gathering:** In this section you will write about what information you chose to use and from where you got the information to include in your work.

- **Creation and development of my piece of work:** In this section you will write about how you created the brochure and how it developed.

- **Checking and saving my work:** In this section you will describe how you checked the accuracy of your work and how you saved it. You will include two printouts of the actual finished brochure. One will be the version which you printed out before having it checked. The second will be the final version which has been checked and corrected.

- **Evaluation:** In this section you will write about how well you did. This will include a description of all the things you had to consider when using IT to produce your brochure.

❯ What you need to do to get the main body of marks

1 When you have chosen your task, load a word processor on your computer and type in the details of the task you are going to do. You will need to write a couple of lines about the car company. You will need to write a brief description about the brochure you are going to produce and what it will look like. Put this under the heading **Introduction**.

2 The next thing you will need to do is to collect some newspaper and magazine cuttings about cars. **At least two** different publications must be used. You will paste these onto paper and put them under the heading **Information gathering**.

You must also collect some information from an IT source. This must, of course, be relevant to your task. In this task you collect information about cars, not just information about anything. It would be best to use clipart from your school network. It is not a good idea to use the Internet just yet as you will need to use it later on for higher marks. **If you don't use another source apart from the Internet you can only get 13 marks**. The solution is therefore to use clipart from your school network or a CD-ROM at this stage and not use clipart from the Internet. Print out some images of cars, saying where they came from and put these under the heading **Information gathering**.

3 The next stage is to use some of this information to create your brochure. Because we are only talking about low marks here, you only have to produce two or three pages for your brochure. You could produce a front cover with a picture of a car and the name of the showroom. You could produce two more pages with pictures of cars and some writing about them. You should print these out and include them in your **Creation and development of my piece of work** section. You need to write on the printouts which information was copied and pasted and from where it was copied.

Ordinary Car Company

I copied this from the cars section on our schools Clipart CD-ROM and pasted it here on my front cover.

✔ A D V I C E

Doing all of numbers 1 to 3 will give you a mark of 2 if you have done them correctly. Your teacher may give you only 1 mark if you have done them all but you have not done them particularly well.

4 So far you have created three pages. On the second and third pages you should have included pictures of cars with some text. You need to have at least two images and two pieces of text. For the next mark range you must include at least two examples of numbers. A good idea is to use a list of car prices to show you have used the decimal point or commas and currency symbol correctly. On a fourth page you could put a list of cars you have collected from your magazines or newspapers.

Make	Model	Price
Smart	City	£6,999
Mazda	MX-5	£8,999
MG	TF 135 Spark	£16,451
Ford	StreetKa	£11,999
Lotus	Elise	£22,999

This list has been created using a left tab for the model and a decimal tab for the price. The commas are all in line and so the numbers have clearly been formatted appropriately. Print out your list and write briefly about how you produced it under the heading **Creation and development of my piece of work**.

5 The other thing you must do for a mark in the range 3–4 is to show how your work has developed. To do this you will need to produce at least three printouts of your work showing how it developed.

You could show how your second page developed by getting three printouts like this:

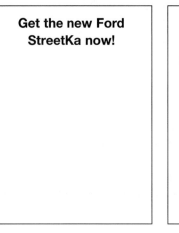

Get the new Ford StreetKa now!

Get the new Ford StreetKa now!

Get the new Ford StreetKa now!

This new model has a 1600 cc engine producing 95 bhp

You must write about how you created this page:

- the type of fonts or font sizes you used;
- where you got your picture from and how you inserted it;
- creating a text box and typing in the text at the bottom.

Put all this in your section **Creation and development of my piece of work**.

6 Now you need to write down the reason for producing your brochure. You will write about why the brochure is needed. You must identify an audience. For example, you may write about the car showroom needing to attract single people in their 20s. It could be that the manager of the showroom is worried about the fact that the showroom doesn't sell many cars to people in this age range. In your write-up make a list of features of this type of audience and what type of car and what type of advertising might appeal to this age range.

You could write about how this audience might prefer fast, two-seater cars as they are single and don't have a family. They would prefer a more modern type of advertising than older, family men or women. You must give examples here of what you would expect to see in terms of types of images (give examples of images which would appeal to younger adults) and the wording of the brochure (not exactly slang, but certainly not too formal). Of course you would have to write about a different type of advertising if the audience was a different age range. Type all this under the heading **Introduction**.

7 You have to show that you have thought about different layouts. There are two ways of doing this.

Before you started producing your brochure you probably drew two or three layouts of the brochure. You should put these in the first part of your **Creation and development of my piece of work** section. You should write down which one you decided to use and why you think it's the best.

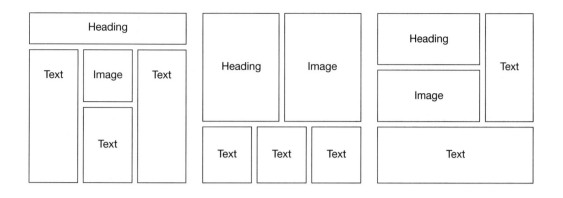

The alternative way of doing it is to change the layout as you develop your brochure. You could move the text, images and numbers around the page to different positions. You must get printouts of these different layouts. When you have got them in the position you think is best you will need to write about which layout is best and say why. Put all these printouts after your previous work under the heading **Creation and development of my piece of work**.

One example could be like this but you will need more than one example of changing the layout.

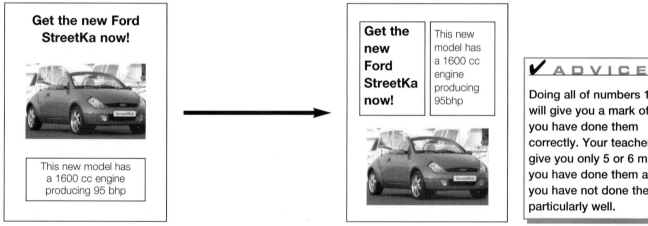

ADVICE

Doing all of numbers 1 to 7 will give you a mark of 7 if you have done them correctly. Your teacher may give you only 5 or 6 marks if you have done them all but you have not done them particularly well.

8 In your work for Step 5, you showed how your work had developed. Now you must write down the reasons why you developed it the way you did. You will write about how these changes suit the audience you are aiming the work at. You may well have made an image bigger or changed the font to one you think your audience would prefer. These must be appropriate reasons. You cannot invent reasons. You can either:

• write the reasons on the printouts of your development in the **Creation and development of my piece of work** section.

Or

• type them up on a separate page, print it out and put it after the printouts of your development in the **Creation and development of my piece of work** section.

You will need to give reasons for each development or change you made.

9 You must make sure that the look of your brochure is consistent. In your brochure you must have used the same font for each description of a car. You must make sure the pictures of cars are in the same position on each page and are the same size. For example, if you set out one page like the one in Step 5, above, you must set out all your pages like this, except, perhaps, for the front and back pages.

To get a mark of 11 or more you will need to produce a significant piece of work. You must create at least eight A5 or A4 pages of a document or eight slides in a presentation.

If you want to gain marks above 13 you must use more than one IT source. If you have just used clipart from a CD (not the Internet) or photos taken using a digital camera in your work so far, you will now need to use a source which lets you search for information. You should choose the Internet or a CD-ROM encyclopaedia. **It is important to understand that the Internet counts as only one source**. If you have not followed the advice given in 2 above and instead used the Internet to find pictures and clipart, you will now need to use a CD-ROM encyclopaedia.

Until now you might have produced a brochure with only three or four pages. You must now make sure that your final brochure has at least eight pages when you finish. These eight pages should include work from the Internet for marks above 14.

10 If you have produced a brochure with only three or four pages, you must add at least four more pages to it. You need to show the development of two or three of these additional pages. Print them out like you did for Step 5 above and add them to your **Creation and development of my piece of work** section. Remember to add reasons to Step 6 saying why you think an eight-page brochure is needed for your audience. This should be added to what you already have written in your **Introduction** section. You will need to add to Step 8 your reasons for developing the extra pages to suit your audience. This goes in your **Creation and development of my piece of work** section.

11 When you have finished your brochure you must check the accuracy of each page of the brochure. There are two ways you can do this. Whichever one you use, you must have a printout showing the brochure containing the mistakes you made before it was checked.

One way is to get a critical adult to proofread your work. The adult will check for grammatical, spelling and factual mistakes. They must write on your work where they find any mistakes. You will need to make sure they write their comments down and put their signature underneath. You must correct any mistakes and print out the corrected version. If there are spelling or grammar mistakes in your brochure you will not get a mark in the 11–13 range. Remember, this is **not** an evaluation of your brochure. The proofreader must comment on the accuracy of the information contained in your brochure. The proofreader is not required to comment on how nice the brochure looks or make any comments on how it could be improved by changing colours, fonts etc. Don't forget to say who is doing the proofreading and to put a line or two of writing to describe each printout. Put this part of your write-up under a new heading, **Checking and saving my work**.

The other way of checking your work is to use a spelling and grammar checker. You will need to show printouts to prove you have done this.

You must:
- print out your booklet *before* checking your spelling;
- use a spellchecker and correct your spelling mistakes;
- print a screen dump showing the spellchecker;
- print out the booklet again.

Make	Model	Price
Smart	Citiy	£6,999
Mazda	MX-5	£8,999
MG	TF 135 Spark	£16,451
Lotus	Elise	£22,999

Spelling and Grammar: English (U.K.)

Not in Dictionary:

Smart **Citiy** £6,999

Suggestions:

Citify
City
Cite

Screenshot of spellchecker

If you have decided to use a spellchecker, your printouts and write-up must go in the **Checking and saving my work** section.

12 You will also need to show you have saved your work properly. You should have created a new folder called **ICT GCSE coursework**. Inside this folder you should have created a new folder called **Project 1a**. Inside this folder you must save your brochure together with the different stages of your work. You will not get a mark in the 11–13 range if you have called your work 'Chelsea', 'Arsenal', 'McFly', 'Christine Aguilera' etc.

You will need printouts of the screen showing your folders and the names of the booklet documents you have saved.

ols Help

Search   Folders

brochure write
up   car brochure
v1   car brochure
v2   car

Screenshot of coursework folder

✔ **A D V I C E**

Doing all of numbers 1 to 12 will give you a mark of 13 if you have done them correctly. Your teacher may give you only 11 or 12 marks if you have done them all but you have not done them particularly well.

13 In order to get higher marks than 13 you must prove that you have used more than one IT source. You will probably use the Internet as one IT source. You must provide evidence that you have used another source such as clipart from a disc, scanned images, CD-ROMs or digital cameras. If you have scanned one of your non-IT pictures you can **NOT** count this as both an IT and a non-IT source. The best advice is to use clipart provided by your teacher or from a CD-ROM or to use scanned images *provided by your teacher*. You will need to show screenshots showing how these were used. You must write about how you used this source. If the Internet is your second source, then if you follow the advice for 14 below, this will provide the evidence you need. Put these printouts and your write-up about what you have done under the heading **Information gathering**.

14 Now you must get a screenshot of a search you have used on the Internet. It must use AND or OR or NOT. You could have typed in 'two seater cars' for your search. You will not have got the results you wanted. The first site is a site for making cars from kits which is not what you want. If you type in 'two seater cars NOT kit' it will remove this type of site. Write about which search engine you used and how you changed the search criteria. Put the screenshots and your write-up under the heading **Information gathering**.

two seater cars		two seater cars NOT kit
SEARCH: ○ Worldwide ◉ United Kingdom RESULTS IN:		SEARCH: ○ Worldwide ◉ United Kingdom RESULTS IN:

AltaVista found 179,000 results About

Sports **Cars**, Lightweight, **Two Seater**, Kit
... Kellysearch for Sports **Cars**, Lightweight, **Two Seater**, Kit - **cars** from Toyota. Try the 225-hp Solara SE Sport or the racing m
www.kellysearch.com/gb-product-86885.html
More pages from kellysearch.com

smart car - the innovative stylish car from DaimlerChrysler
- the classic model - 50 or 61 bhp turbo engine - ESP and Ab electric windows - remote central locking. The full story on this tu turbo engine - " sportline" alloy wheels -
www.thesmart.co.uk/smart_range/cars/coupe/index.asp
More pages from thesmart.co.uk

Morgan **Cars** Brochure - 4/4
Technical. specifications. The Morgan 4/4 is a **two-seater** sports from the mediocre.
www.bhm.uk.com/brochure2001/morgan4+4.htm

Lycos - Grand Legend **Two Seater** 4x4 Jeep in Bobby Prices and Buy
Grand Legend **Two Seater** 4x4 Jeep buy from Prezzybox at L minute to think back to when you were a 3 year old rascal. Of few years ago for some ... Leisure » ... » Outdoor Toys & Child Legend **Two Seater** 4x4 Jeepat Prezzybox insure buy ... we p 'Grand Legend'.The Grand Legend ...
shopping.lycos.co.uk/3717en1891.html
More pages from shopping.lycos.co.uk

BBC SPORT | Motorsport | Formula One | Minardi float **tw**
... boss Paul Stoddart claims four F1 teams have agreed to c Grand Prix weekends ... the plan would see 10 **cars** lining up in t news.bbc.co.uk/sport1/hi/motorsport/formula_one/3421645.stm
More pages from news.bbc.co.uk

RIDE IN A **TWO SEATER** GIFT IDEAS EXPERIENC

15 You will now click on some of these hyperlinks and go to the web sites. You need to show screenshots of at least three different sites. You will choose some of the pictures or text that you think are suitable. You will write about how you downloaded images or text to your work area. Obviously you must now include some of these in your brochure and say why you chose some of the images or text and not others. The reasons you give must be because they suit your audience. Remember, you cannot just use phrases like 'I have chosen this picture because I think it suits my audience'. You must say **why** you think it suits your audience. Print out the images or text you have used and one or two examples of those you haven't. It will be easier if you write on these printouts why you did (or didn't) choose them rather than doing a separate write-up. Put these in your **Creation and development of my piece of work** section.

16 For 15 above you probably showed evidence of using three different hyperlinks. This was presumably because you thought the hyperlinks you followed were most suitable. You need to write about which hyperlinks appeared to be suitable for your purpose or audience. You are trying to sell cars to young adults. You might write that you think a hyperlink describing how to pay for a Formula 1 car ride might not suit your purpose. You must write about which hyperlinks you thought would be most suitable and which would not. The reasons you give must be about how they match your ideas about what your audience would want.

Put this part of your write-up in your **Information gathering** section.

17 For 15 above you downloaded some images or text to put in your brochure. To get a mark of more than 16 you must show how you formatted the image or text before putting it into your brochure. You must print out the original and then you must print out the new, formatted version. You could crop an image or change the font and font size of some text. Put these in your **Creation and development of my piece of work** section.

18 You will need to provide evidence that new information has been produced. This is done by changing information obtained from one of your sources. You must use a separate software package to do this. For example, you could download some text from the Internet into a word processing package. You could then change it into your own words to simplify and summarise the text. Alternatively, you could download some prices of cars into a spreadsheet. You could then use formulae to find things like the average price, the most expensive car or the cheapest (using Average, Maximum, Minimum functions) or produce a graph of prices. You will not get full marks if you simply copy down prices from different parts of a site. This derived information must be as a result of changing imported or downloaded information. It must then be imported or inserted into your brochure. You must print out a copy of the original information and a copy of the new information. You must write about how you changed it. The printouts and your write-up go at the end of your **Creation and development of my piece of work** section.

19 To gain full marks you have to use a spell-checker **and** a proof-reader. Look at point II, above, to remind yourself what you should do.

✔ A D V I C E

Doing all of numbers 1 to 19 will give you a mark of 21 if you have done them correctly. Your teacher may give you only 20 marks if you have done them all but you have not done them particularly well.

❯ What you need to do to get the 'Additional Skills' marks

You should use your own work to give examples for all the Additional Skills marks.

1 You must write about how you used IT to make your brochure. You will need to write about how you could have used another way of making the brochure. You could have done it all by hand and cut out magazine pictures and glued them in. You do not have to write too much but you must write about how using IT made it easier. It would be a good idea to write about how hard it would be to draw pictures of cars if you are not very good at Art. Write about how your handwriting is not very neat. You would then say how a brochure produced on a word processor would be neater. Put this in your **Evaluation** section.

2 You must now write about how you have worked safely. You will have some safety rules in your computer room. You must say how you have kept to the rules while you were producing your brochure. Add this to your **Evaluation** section.

3 The next thing is to show that you know how to look after equipment in the computer room. You should write a list of things that you have done whilst working in the computer room. You could write about how you used a floppy disc to carry work back and forward from school to home. You could add that you never carried it in your pockets and give the reason why. Add this to your **Evaluation** section.

4 Now write about how you made backups. You may have used floppy discs, CD-ROMs or memory sticks to make a backup. Get a screenshot of a window showing your work folders with your backups on it. Add this to your **Evaluation** section.

5 You must show that you got help when you saw error messages. You will need to print out screenshots of error messages. Then, you will write about how you used the on-line help or asked a teacher or technician. Put this in your **Evaluation** section.

**✔ A D V I C E**

Doing all of numbers 1 to 5 will give you a mark of 2 if you have done them correctly. Your teacher may give you only 1 mark if you have done them all but you have not done them particularly well.

6 You must now write down two advantages and two disadvantages of using IT. These must be advantages and disadvantages that you have found while creating your brochure. An example of one advantage is the way that you can change information on a computer. You can do this without having to write or type it all out again. You will need to get a printout of your work with some mistakes and then a printout showing how you corrected them. You would write about how this is easier than copying it all out again. A disadvantage might be that you can sometimes have a system crash which means you lose your work. You will need to write about this and how you lost some work when creating your brochure. You could write about how this is less likely to happen if you do not use a computer. Add this to your **Evaluation** section.

7 Next you must write about copyright or confidentiality. You could write that it is illegal to use copyright material without the owner's permission. You could write about how personal information should not be made public. You only need to give an example of one of these. Print out one of the images which you probably did not use from the Internet because of copyright issues. Add this to your **Evaluation** section.

8 This follows on from Step 5 above. You need to get a screenshot of the error message and write about what caused it. Here is an example of an error message that might happen. You would write about what caused this and then write about what you could do to correct it.

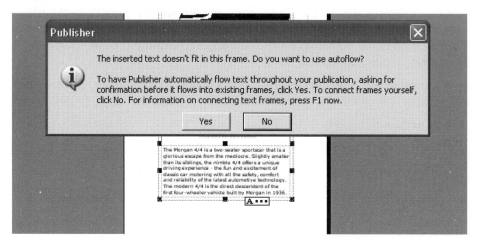

Put the printouts and your write-up in your **Evaluation** section.

9 Now you need to write about virus prevention. You should give some examples of what you did in the course of producing your brochure. Screenshots of a virus checker in progress would be very good evidence here. Other examples need to be given and must be related to your own work.

10 Now you must write a few lines about each of two health issues. You could write about how you always sat properly when creating your brochure in order to reduce backache.

An example project

Here is a project which achieved a mark of 26. The pupil was awarded 19 of the main marks and 7 for the Additional Skills marks. Here is a list of the criteria for 17 to 19 main marks and where they were met in the project.

Use a computer to develop a significant piece of work using different types of information from a range of IT sources and non-IT sources.	Brochure and Printouts on Page 19 Pages 1–9 of write-up
State the purpose of the work.	Page 1 of write-up
Write down how the development matches the purpose of the work.	Pages 8–13
Search for information using multiple criteria.	Page 3
Use hyperlinks or refined searches to identify information which is suitable for the purpose of the work.	Pages 4, 5
Use editing techniques to bring in some of the information.	Page 8
Use formatting techniques to bring in some of the information.	Pages 10–13
Experiment with layouts and choose an appropriate layout for the selected information.	Page 5
Include text, images and numbers in the work.	Brochure and write-up Pages 5–13 (number is explained on page 9)
Show consistency throughout the work.	Brochure Printouts on Page 19
Use a spellchecker or proofreader to check the accuracy of the work.	Pages 13, 14
Save information using appropriate folders and file names	Page 15

The project could not achieve a higher mark as the pupil did not use a proofreader. If he/she had used one then the proofreader would no doubt have picked up on words like 'sped' and 'voce' (page 7 of the brochure) which the spellchecker failed to pick up. Technically, you could say that they are correctly spelt but they do not make sense grammatically and are incorrect versions of 'speed' and 'voice'. The screen dump of the copyright warning (page 23 of the write-up) has been omitted to prevent plagiarism by students. It would also be expected that a printout showing errors and a printout showing corrections would be included.

Here is a list of the criteria for the Additional Skills marks and where they were met in the project.

Can write about the advantages and disadvantages of using IT.	Pages 15, 16
Can work safely and take care of equipment and avoid losing information	Page 16
Can identify errors and their causes.	Page 17
Knows how to minimise risks from viruses.	Page 18
Knows how to minimise health risks.	Page 18
Knows when it is necessary to observe copyright or confidentiality.	Page 18

■ Introduction

Phones4each is a local company which sells mobile phones. They have done a survey and found that they are not selling many phones to businessmen in their twenties or thirties. They think that this is a mistake as people of this type could spend lots of money on phones.

I'm going to produce a booklet which will advertise the company to this type of audience. It will have several pages in it with pictures of phones and some writing about each one. The pictures and text will be chosen to suit this type of audience. I am going to keep it at A5 size so that it is not too big for people to carry around. A younger audience would need to know all about the different ring tones, the type of camera or video the phone has and the number of games you can have. My audience won't want to know all this, as they'll just be using it for business they won't have time for all the rest. The images would probably be better for a young audience if they were modern, colourful and like cartoons. My audience will want to see actual photos of the camera and won't want it too jazzed up.

■ Sources of Information

Here are some cut outs from the ***** ******* newspaper.

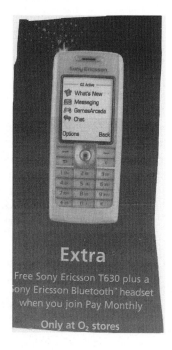

Here is a page from ✱ ✱ ✱ ✱ ✱ ✱ magazine:

Here are some photos from clipart which I found in the 'GCSE project 1a resources'
folder on our school network.

■ Use of the Internet

I used mainly clipart and scanned images for my four-page booklet but I thought it was a bit short. I decided to use the Internet to add a few more pages. I went on to Altavista.co.uk to find more information and pictures. I typed in 'mobile + phones' to see what would come up. The '+' is the same as typing in the Boolean AND.

This is what happened:

It looked as though there were plenty of free offers and such like but not things that would interest my audience of young businessmen. I then typed in 'mobile+phones+business' to give me more accurate results.

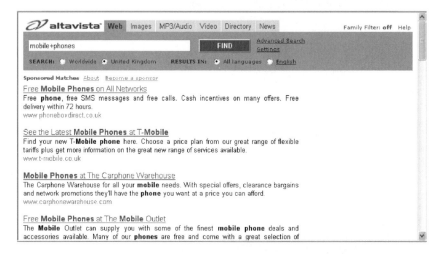

At first it looked like I had got some good results:

When I went to some of the hyperlinks it wasn't so good:

Reduce Business **Mobile** Costs

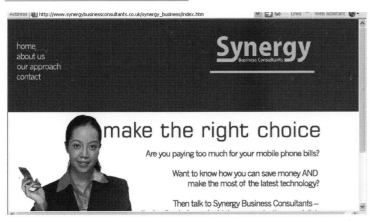

This wasn't going to give me much information about different phones. It is mainly about giving business services.

Cut Your UK Company **Mobile Phone** Costs

This was their page on mobile phones. There wasn't much information about phones here.

Mobile Phone Packages For Business

This was the best site yet. It had pictures of phones and details about phone plans.

This one was advertising business plans.

Active Digital

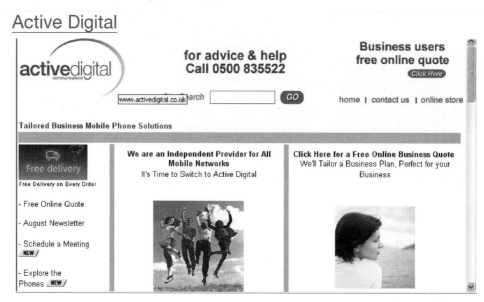

Links 1, 2 and 4 on Altavista are giving business advice but not much details about phone plans. Link 3 is all about business phones so I will use that one. I looked at the three deals they were offering. I then developed my brochure using information from the three deals.

■ Creation and development of my piece of work

These were my first ideas for the layout of the front page

Name of company
Picture
Text

Name of company	
Issue No.	Text
Picture	

Name of company (side ways)	Issue no./date
	Picture
	Text

Spring 2005 Brochure

Phones4each

Come to Phones4each for personal attention.

We stock all the latest phones together with all the latest payment plans.

We will make sure you walk away with the best phone and pay plan for your needs!

1

I decided on the third layout because I didn't want to make the company name the first thing anyone saw when they picked up the booklet. It needed to be there but to the side. As it is an advertising brochure and there won't be that many I thought it would be silly to have an issue number. I put the season at the top so that readers would know whether they'd got the up to date version. The space next to the company name is smaller than the space underneath. I'm going to put the picture there and leave the bigger space for any writing about the company.

Here are the next two pages of my brochure:

Phones4each

At Phones4each we find this is one of the most popular phones for only £135.99

Motorola V500

- Picture caller id
- Extensive memory
- Quad band
- Integrated camera
- Recordable voice memo

2

Phones4each

At Phones4each we find this is one of the best pay plans at just £15.99 per month

Vodafone

- Free Sony Ericsson K700i
- 600 minutes a month
- 250 free texts a month

3

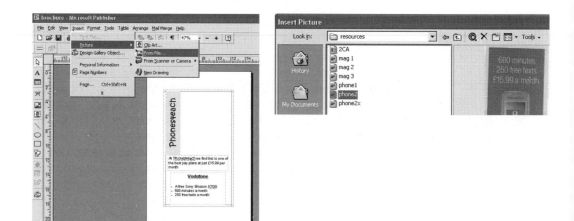

To get the phone on page 3 I scanned the newspaper photograph into my computer and saved it as Phone 2. I then loaded my phone booklet in Publisher, went to Insert and clicked on 'Picture' and then 'From File'. I went to my folder called 'Resources' and clicked on 'Phone 2'. I cropped it so that the writing was deleted.

To make my booklet I used Microsoft Publisher and chose 'blank publications' and 'book fold'. I changed it to landscape so that the pages wouldn't be too narrow. To make my first page I clicked on the WordArt icon and drew a box.

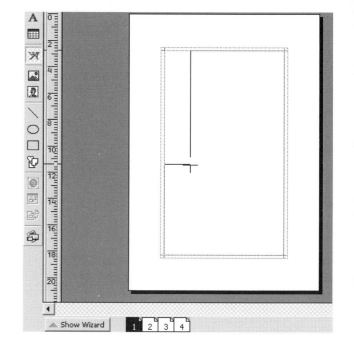

Then I typed in Phones4each, changed the font to Kristen ITC and clicked on the rotate button and changed it to 90°.

Then I clicked on the grey space.

I then clicked on the fill icon and chose yellow for the background. This will be my Logo.

I chose a logo like this because of the age group and the type of person I am aiming to attract. Younger people might not be impressed by having this type of house style but I am sure businessmen would like it because it makes the look a lot more professional.

The next step was to create a text frame and put the date in. As the company would only need four per year I am only giving the name of the season. I chose Ariel as the font and a pink background.

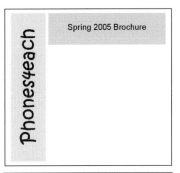

Next I put in a photograph from Clip art. I clicked on Insert. I went to the clipart gallery, typed in phones and this was one of the photographs that came up. I clicked on it and then clicked on the Insert clip icon. I chose to add this photograph because, again, it gives the image of a smart young businessman. The other photographs were not suitable as they were just a phone or pictures of someone in a car. This photograph has pictures of lots of office blocks in the background and seemed to represent business.

Then I made a text box and typed in some information about the company. I changed the font for Phones4each to Kristen ITC to make it the same as the logo. I chose Arial for the rest of the text as it is formal, which businessmen would like, but not too formal like Times New Roman which would also be a little old-fashioned for this audience.

At Phones4each we find this is one of the most popular phones for only £223.99

Panasonic X70

- Photo light
- Self-timer
- Blue tooth wireless technology
- Downloadable games
- Zoom capability

2

This was my original page 2 but I changed it to the one you see in the final brochure after I had typed in the description. As I said in my introduction, I don't think that young businessmen would be interested in having games or a photo light and self-timer on their camera. The phone I have included instead has a recordable voice memo which business people would find useful. It has quad band which means wherever they are in the world they can use the phone. This would be better for them than having different ring tones and fancy camera tricks. My brochure wants to convince them that this shop caters for businessmen.

On every page I have put the company name as you can see above and on page 4 below.

Massive reductions!

20% off

See below what massive savings you can make when you compare our prices to major catalogue prices!

Phone	Catalogue Price	Our Price
Motorola E365	£129.99	£103.99
Samsung E700	£249.99	£199.99
Motorola V500	£169.99	£135.99
Panasonic X70	£279.99	£223.99

4

For page 4 I copied down the phones and the prices from the magazine.

I put all the prices in line by using the decimal tab function. I worked out what OUR price would be by using the calculator to knock 20% off. I used the decimal tab to put all these in line.

As I said in my second section I used mainly clipart and scanned images for my four page booklet. I decided to use the Internet to add a few more pages. This is how I did it.

Deal 1

I downloaded the text and reformatted it. It was in a table so I changed it into text. Then I changed the font to Arial to match my first three pages and changed the font size to 14 to match my first three pages.

Connect the Sony Ericsson T610 free on Your Plan 400 and receive:

Double Minutes (for 6 months).

25% Line Rental Discount (for 6 months).

Free Bluetooth Headset.

PLUS – a second Sony Ericsson T610 and Bluetooth headset with one years free line rental!

When I clicked on the phone this came up.

Connect the Sony Ericsson T610 free on Your Plan 400 and receive:

Double Minutes (for 6 months).

25% Line Rental Discount (for 6 months).

Free Bluetooth Headset.

PLUS – a second Sony Ericsson T610 and Bluetooth headset with one years free line rental!

I copied the table so I could reformat it. Here is the table.

‹ Telecom : Orange Business Solutions - Microsoft In... ▫

Phone Specifications...

Sony Ericsson T610

Battery life:
• Talk time 5.0 hours
• Standby 8.0 days

Weight: 95g

Features:
• Bluetooth technology
• Built-in camera
• Calculator
• Colour screen
• Composable ring tones
• Date/clock/alarm
• Downloadable games
• Email
• GPRS
• GPRS and HSCSD
• Infrared connection
• Java™ capable
• Phone book memory
• Photo Messaging
• Polyphonic ring tones
• Selection of games
• Tri band technology
• Wap

102.0mm

19.0mm   44.0mm

Sony Ericsson T610
Battery life: • **Talk time 5.0 hours**   • **Standby 8.0 days**
Weight: **95g**
Features: • **Bluetooth technology**   • **Built-in camera**   • **Calculator**   • **Colour screen**   • **Composable ring tones**   • **Date/clock/alarm**   • **Downloadable games**   • **Email**   • **GPRS**   • **GPRS and HSCSD**   • **Infrared connection**   • **Java™ capable**   • **Phone book memory**   • **Photo Messaging**   • **Polyphonic ring tones**   • **Selection of games**   • **Tri band technology**   • **Wap**

I changed the table to text. I changed the font and font size and made it not bold.

Sony Ericsson T610

Battery life:

- **Talk time 5.0 hours**
- **Standby 8.0 days**

Weight: 95g

Features:
- **Bluetooth technology**
- **Built-in camera**
- **Calculator**
- **Colour screen**
- **Date/clock/alarm**
- **Email**
- **GPRS and HSCSD**
- **Infrared connection**
- **Phone book memory**
- **Tri band technology**
- **Wap**

Sony Ericsson T610

Battery life:

- Talk time 5.0 hours
- Standby 8.0 days

Weight: 95g

Features:
- Bluetooth technology
- Built-in camera
- Calculator
- Colour screen
- Date/clock/alarm
- Email
- GPRS and HSCSD
- Infrared connection
- Phone book memory
- Tri band technology
- Wap

Because I want it to appeal to businessmen, I left out all the details which were not to do with business. I also changed the features into my own words.

Features:

You get all the normal features like camera, date, clock, colour screen and phone book. In addition you get to be able to use this phone anywhere in the world. You can download at ten times the normal speed using new GPRS technology.

Then I copied the picture of the phone and the two pieces of text and pasted it into my booklet.

Deal 2

The next link I followed was to deal 2.

I copied most of the text and then reformatted it, getting rid of some of the text which wouldn't apply to the young businessman. I thought that if there were 50 workers the company would be too big to deal with Phones4each.

Connect 50 users to Orange Business Talk Plans and reduce the standard annual line rental by over £7000.

The handset shown is the Nokia 3510i but other handsets are available, please contact us for further details.

Get more for your money with
Business Standards ...

Save up to 50% on your plan.

Free phone insurance.

Free mobile fax number.

Free answer phone retrieval.

Orange text alerts.

The handset shown is the Nokia 3510i but other handsets are available, please contact us for further details.

Save up to 50% on your plan.

→ Free phone insurance.

Free mobile fax number.

Free answer phone retrieval.

Orange text alerts.

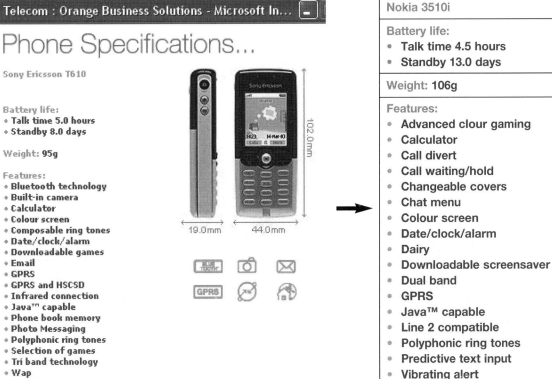

Telecom : Orange Business Solutions - Microsoft In...

Phone Specifications...

Sony Ericsson T610

Battery life:
• Talk time 5.0 hours
• Standby 8.0 days

Weight: 95g

Features:
• Bluetooth technology
• Built-in camera
• Calculator
• Colour screen
• Composable ring tones
• Date/clock/alarm
• Downloadable games
• Email
• GPRS
• GPRS and HSCSD
• Infrared connection
• Java™ capable
• Phone book memory
• Photo Messaging
• Polyphonic ring tones
• Selection of games
• Tri band technology
• Wap

19.0mm   44.0mm   102.0mm

Nokia 3510i
Battery life: • **Talk time 4.5 hours** • **Standby 13.0 days**
Weight: **106g**
Features: • **Advanced clour gaming** • **Calculator** • **Call divert** • **Call waiting/hold** • **Changeable covers** • **Chat menu** • **Colour screen** • **Date/clock/alarm** • **Dairy** • **Downloadable screensaver** • **Dual band** • **GPRS** • **Java™ capable** • **Line 2 compatible** • **Polyphonic ring tones** • **Predictive text input** • **Vibrating alert** • **Wap**

I copied the table and changed it to text and changed the font and font size and then changed it into my own words –

Advanced colour gaming
Calculator
Call divert
Call waiting/hold
Changeable covers
Chat menu
Colour screen
Date/clock/alarm
Diary
Downloadable screensaver
Dual band
GPRS
Java™ capable
Line 2 compatible
Polyphonic ring tones
Predictive text input
Vibrating alert
Wap

Features:

You get a calculator, call divert, call hold, date, clock, colour screen and diary. You can use this phone in most countries in the world. The phone vibrates so you can take calls without interrupting meetings. You can download at ten times the normal speed using new GPRS technology.

I then did the same for deal 3.

To make my 7th page I went on the Internet and found a site called Onetel and got details about the Siemens MC60 from there.

■ Checking and saving my work

After I had finished my booklet I used the spellchecker to check the accuracy of it.

All the mistakes that came up were problems with things like the name of the company:

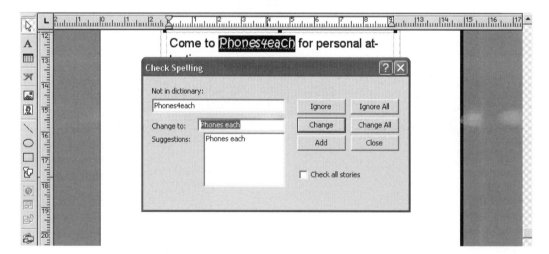

Words like recordable:

The makes, such as Vodafone:

Other words which came up were words like 'colourful'. This was because the spellchecker was looking for American words and not English.

Here is a real mistake that it found:

I changed it to 'countries' as you can see in my finished work.

Here are screenshots of my work:

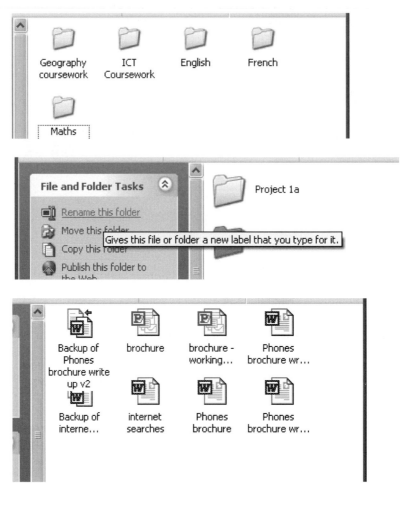

■ Evaluation

■ Advantages and Disadvantages

One advantage of producing my brochure using IT was that it was easier to make my book look professional. I am not very good with my hands, and to position the Phones4each logo and the photographs and glue them down exactly where I wanted them would have been very difficult. With Publisher I just used the size and position option on the Format menu.

Another advantage was that when I used the spellchecker and found I had typed in 'countries' wrong I just clicked on 'change'. I didn't have to do that page all over again.

One disadvantage I found was that I couldn't put the writing to the right of the pictures and underneath. It all had to go to the right and I had to leave a gap underneath the picture. If I had done it manually I could have carried on the writing from 'use this' and carried on under the picture.

Features:
You get all the normal features like camera, date, clock, colour screen and phone book. In addition you get to be able to use this phone anywhere in the world. You can download at ten times the normal speed using new GPRS technology.

One other disadvantage was that the scanned pictures weren't as good quality as the originals. If I had done it manually I could have used the originals.

Safety and looking after equipment

When I was using the computers I always made sure that I didn't eat or drink in the computer room. If I saw any trailing wires I always told the technician or the teacher. I never moved the monitor in case it caused the plug to come loose in the socket. I never carried floppy disks in my pockets in case they got fluff in them and did not work and I was always careful not to slam the mouse down or type in to the keyboard too hard.

Below you can see the proof that I made backups of my files.

Backups

Errors and Their Causes

It is important to use the on-line help that Office gives you if you make an error. One problem I had was when I copied text from the Internet. I copied it all at once the first time and this happened:

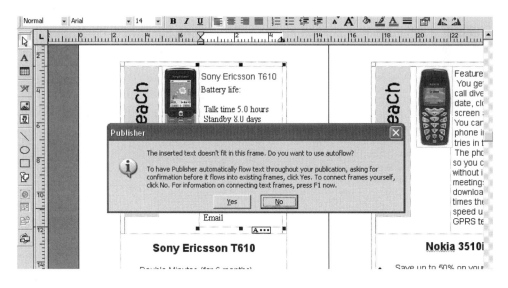

The amount of text was too much for the frame.

I didn't want my text flowing on to another page so I went back and edited it in Word before putting it back in Publisher when it was small enough to fit.

Another error I kept on getting was from the automatic spellchecker. It puts a squiggly red line underneath any word that it thinks isn't spelt properly. To correct it you just press F7.

Features:

You get a calculator, call divert, call hold, date, clock, colour screen and diary. You can use this phone in most countries in the world. The phone vibrates so you can take calls without interrupting meetings. You can download at ten times the normal speed using new GPRS technology.

Then you choose whether you want to change or not. I ignored it.

Health

I know that regular use of computers can cause headaches and eyestrain so I never used the computer for more than one hour at a time. I would then take a rest and watch television or something at a further distance than the computer screen.

Sitting at the computer can also cause back strain so I always tried to keep my back straight and never slouched in front of the computer.

Viruses

To make sure my work didn't get viruses I used Norton Antivirus to scan my floppy discs. I also never downloaded attachments to emails or software from the Internet.

Here is Norton working:

Copyright

Copyright is the right of someone to protect their work. If you write or record something, people are not allowed to copy it without your permission. This also applies to stuff you put on the Internet. If you want to use somebody else's work you must get their permission first.

Here is a screenshot of a warning about the clipart I used. It says I can't use it for 'monetary gain' but I am not using it to make money so that is okay.

My finished brochure:

Spring 2005 Brochure

Come to Phones4each for personal attention.

We stock all the latest phones together with all the latest payment plans.

We will make sure you walk away with the best phone and pay plan for your needs!

At Phones4each we find this is one of the most popular phones for only £135.99.

Motorola V500

- Picture caller id
- Extensive memory
- Quad band
- Integrated camera
- Recordable voice memo

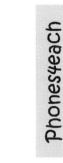

At Phones4each we find this is one of the best pay plans at just £15.99 per month.

Vodafone

- Free Sony Ericsson K700i
- 600 minutes a month
- 250 free texts a month

Features:
You get all the normal features like camera, date, clock, colour screen and phone book. In addition you get to be able to use this phone anywhere in the world. You can download at then time the normal speed using new GPRS technology.

Sony Ericsson T610

- Double Minutes (for 6 months)
- 25% Line Rental Discount (6 months)
- Free Bluetooth Headset
- PLUS – a second Sony Ericsson T610 and Bluetooth headset with one year's free line rental!

Features:
You get a calculator, call divert, call hold, date, clock, colour screen and diary. You can use this phone in most countries in the world. The phone vibrates so you can take calls without interrupting meetings. You can download at ten times the normal speed using new GPRS technology.

Nokia 3510i

- Save up to 50% on your plan
- Free phone insurance
- Free mobile fax number
- Free answer phone retrieval
- Orange text alerts

Features:
You get all the normal features like camera, date, clock, colour screen and phone book. In addition you get to be able to use this phone anywhere in the world. You can download at ten time the normal speed using new GPRS technology.

Nokia 5140

- Improved durability
- Thermometer
- Flashlight
- Digital compass
- FREE Double Minutes for 6 months

Features:
You get a camera. You can use this phone in nearly all countries in the world. The phone vibrates so you can take calls without interrupting meetings. You can download at ten time the normal speed using new GPRS technology. You can use voice activated dialling for safe driving.

Siemens MC60

- Digital imaging
- Picture messaging
- 4K colour screen
- Voice activated dialling

Massive reductions!

20% off

See below what massive savings you can make when you compare our prices to major catalogue prices!

Phone	Catalogue Price	Our Price
Motorola E365	£129.99	£103.99
Samsung E700	£249.99	£199.99
Motorola V500	£169.99	£135.99
Panasonic X70	£279.99	£223.99

If you are doing project 1b using the Handling Data strand, you will need to use a database. First of all we will look at what you must do to get 10 marks for this project. Here are the things you have to do to get the first four mark boxes:

1 Look at the data stored in a database, find answers to questions using the data in the database.

Doing this will give you a mark of 2 if you have done it correctly.

2 Sort the database into order.

Doing numbers 1 and 2 will give you a mark of 4 if you have done them correctly. Your teacher may give you only 3 marks if you have done them both but you have not done them particularly well.

3 Change some of the data in the database when appropriate.

Doing **all** of numbers 1 to 3 will give you a mark of 7 if you have done them correctly. Your teacher may give you only 5 or 6 marks if you have done them all but you have not done them particularly well.

4 Ask people questions to get more data to add to the database and add this new data to the database.

Doing **all** of numbers 1 to 4 will give you a mark of 10 if you have done them correctly. Your teacher may give you only 8 or 9 marks if you have done them all but you have not done them particularly well.

Here is a database called 'Houses'.

Area	Type of house	Bedrooms	Garden	Garage	Value of house	Year house was built
Central	Flat	1	No	Yes	£76,000.00	1999
Central	Flat	2	No	No	£85,000.00	1954
North	Terraced	2	Yes	No	£43,000.00	1932
South	Terraced	3	Yes	No	£35,000.00	1915
East	Semi-detached	3	Yes	No	£45,000.00	1990
West	Semi-detached	3	Yes	Yes	£65,000.00	1968
South	Terraced	3	Yes	No	£55,000.00	1923
Central	Terraced	3	Yes	No	£78,000.00	1958
Central	Flat	3	No	Yes	£95,000.00	1992
South	Detached	3	Yes	Yes	£75,000.00	1987
West	Terraced	3	Yes	No	£45,000.00	1923
North	Semi-detached	3	Yes	Yes	£56,000.00	1966
South	Detached	3	Yes	Yes	£68,000.00	1942
West	Semi-detached	3	Yes	No	£62,000.00	1956
West	Detached	4	Yes	Yes	£70,000.00	1986
Central	Detached	4	Yes	Yes	£125,000.00	1962
North	Semi-detached	4	Yes	Yes	£75,000.00	1968
West	Detached	4	Yes	Yes	£115,000.00	1988
South	Terraced	4	Yes	No	£66,000.00	1932
Central	Flat	4	No	No	£105,000.00	1966

Here is a series of tasks for you to do so that you can achieve mark boxes 1 to 4. Each task corresponds to a mark range. Task 1 gives you mark range 1, task 2 gives you mark range 2 and so on. Your teacher should create the 'Houses' database so that you can use it to do these tasks.

TASK 1:   Load the 'Houses' database.

Create these queries:

1 Find the properties which have 3 bedrooms.
2 Find the properties which are flats.
3 Find the properties which cost more than £80,000.

Print out the results of these queries.

Make sure your name is on these printouts.

Write on each printout what you searched for.

Write two or three lines about what you did for task 1. Write down what information is being kept in the database and how you searched for three different types of property.

TASK 2:   Load the 'Houses' database.

Print it out.

Now choose one field and sort it into either ascending (going up) or descending order (going down).

Print out the sorted database. Write on this printout which field you have sorted and draw an arrow to it.

Make sure your name is on both printouts.

Write two or three lines about what you did for task 2. Write down which field you sorted into order and whether you did it ascending or descending.

TASK 3:   The estate agent who wrote all the data down for this database has made some mistakes. He has put down some of the flats as having a garage. In fact, none of the flats have got garages.

Change the database so that these mistakes are removed. Print out the new database and write your name on it.

To check that you have done it properly, print out all the flats again. (use the query you created for Task 1, query 2).

Make sure your name is on this printout.

Write two or three lines about what you did for task 3. Write down which records you changed and say why you changed them.

TASK 4:   Now you have got to collect some data yourself. First you will need to create a blank data capture form. You can use a spreadsheet package to do this. Write down the headings from the database on it like this and print it out. Make sure yours has at least ten lines.

Area	Type of house	Bedrooms	Garden	Garage	Value of house	Year house was built

Collect the details of at least ten more houses and write them down on this data capture form. You could get them from local estate agents or from local newspaper advertisements.

Load up the 'Houses' database.

Type in the data you have collected in to the database.

Print out the whole database and write your name on it.

Write two or three lines about what you did for task 4. Write down where you got your information from. Write down how you typed in your new data.

Create two more queries of your own for searching your new version of the database.

Print out the results of these queries.

Make sure your name is on these printouts.

Write on each printout what you searched for.

In order to get a mark higher than 10 out of 28 for this strand you will need to create your own database.

> Suggestions for database tasks

1 Make a database of second-hand vehicles using information from local garage advertisements, leaflets and newspapers. If someone wishes to get details on the availability of certain models they can use the database to find them.

2 Make a database of video tapes using information from local video shops, leaflets and newspapers. This database will help a shop assistant to find a particular video tape as well as keeping a record of whether it is in stock or not.

3 Make a database about all the kings and queens of England. This will help an historian to find out various facts about monarchs.

4 Make a database of clothes using information from local shops, leaflets and catalogues. If someone wishes to get details about certain clothes, the shop assistant can use the database to help the customer find them.

5 Make a database of mobile phones using information from local phone shops, magazines and newspapers. This database will help a shop assistant to find a particular mobile phone as well as keeping a record of whether it is in stock or not.

Your work will need to include:

- a data capture sheet;
- collection and input of data;
- searching of data using Boolean operands;
- checking of data using verification;
- checking of data using validation;
- presentation of results;
- reasons why you chose the database software instead of the alternatives available to you;
- reasons why you have chosen the fields, field types and field lengths for your database.

✔ A D V I C E

For the highest range of marks you will need to include a list of the required output needed to solve your task. You will also have to explain all your work giving reasons why you made the choices you did and these must all relate to the required output. This could be quite tricky. Your teacher will tell you if it is advisable for you to do this.

How to get started

The guidance given here is about the mobile phones task. You must use this as guidance to give you ideas and not just copy it out. That could lose you a lot of marks.

Setting out your work

You need to make your work easy for your teacher to mark and easy for the moderator to read. You will need to write up everything you have done. A good idea is to set out your work in different sections. The headings of each section are as follows:

- **Introduction:** In this section you will need to write a paragraph explaining why the database is needed.

- **Data collection and capture:** In this section you will describe where you got the data for your data capture form (your sources).

- **Design of the database:** In this section you will describe the structure of the database you are going to create.

- **Creation of the database:** Here you will describe how you created your database.

- **Verification:** In this section you will describe how you verified your database.

- **Searches:** In this section you will describe how you searched your database.

- **Validation:** In this section you will describe how you validated your database.

> What you need to do to get the marks

1 When you have chosen your task, load a word processor on your computer and type in the details of the task you are going to do. You will describe the sort of questions or searches that you think people could use your database to answer. In your write-up make a list of searches that you are going to do on the database. Type this under the heading **Introduction**.

   You could explain how the phone shop has to deal with customer queries. You might say that a customer could come in and ask for details of the **Nokia** phones in stock. Make sure that you include customer queries asking about more than one piece of information. For example, one customer might want to know about **Nokia** phones which are **blue**. Another customer might want to know about phones which are **blue** or **red**.

2 The next thing you will need to do is to create a data capture form to collect data for your database. You can use a spreadsheet to create the data capture form. It could look something like this (here only the first three column headings have been filled in – you will need to fill in **all** the column headings on your form – make sure you have between six and eight different columns and 30 records at least):

Make	Model	Colour					

Fill in the data capture form by copying down information about phones from magazines, newspapers, phone shops, etc. Under the heading **Data capture and collection** write about how you made this form. Make sure you put the data capture form in this section.

3 In your **Design of the database** section you should design the database you are going to use. Design your database using a table similar to the one below. Use the column headings on your data capture form for your field names. Write a few lines about how you designed the database and put the table underneath.

Name of field	Data type	Field length	Validation check	Example
Make	Text	14	None	Sony Ericsson

4 Decide which database software you are going to use. Load it on to your computer and create your database. Use the details you put in your design table. Now, type in the data from your data capture form into your database. Don't make up any data. Make sure you use only the data on your data capture form. Under the heading **Creation of the database** write a sentence about the software you have used. You should also write two or three lines about how you used it to create your database. You need to print out a copy of your database and put this in the same section.

5 Look through this printout of the database and check that you have typed the data in exactly as it is on your data capture form. Look for any mistakes you have made. Highlight the mistakes you find (this is called *verification*). You are not allowed to say that you have checked your database and made no mistakes. In your **Verification** section write down what you have done. Remember to include a printout of your database with the mistakes highlighted.

6 Now you need to do some queries. Look at the searches you wrote down in your introduction. Using these searches create your queries or filters on the database and print out the results. Do this for all your searches. On each printout make sure you have written down what you were searching for. In your **Searches** section write down a few lines on the searches you have used and include all your printouts. Write a few lines about how you created your queries or filters. Include printouts of screenshots of at least two of them as evidence.

> ✔ A D V I C E
>
> Doing *all* of numbers 1 to 6 will give you a mark of 13 if you have done them correctly. Your teacher may give you only 11 or 12 marks if you have done them all but you have not done them particularly well.

To get a mark of between 14 and 16 you now need to do everything in Steps 7 to 10 below **as well as** what you have done for 1 to 6 above.

7 You are now going to add some more detail to your **Data collection and capture** section. You should have used at least two different sources for your data. In this section write down the names of the sources where you got your information from. Put copies of these magazines, newspapers or Internet printouts in this section. This is to prove that you have used a range of sources.

8 You need to give the reasons why you chose the fields on your data capture form. Write this down immediately before the data capture form in your **Data collection and capture** section. You can do this by copying out the list of likely questions from customers which you should have made in your **Introduction**. For a phone shop questions could be:

- A customer cannot spend more than £100. What phones are available?
- A customer wants a *blue Nokia* phone. What phones are there?

These two questions alone tell you that you need fields for PRICE (£100), COLOUR (blue) and MAKE (Nokia). Other questions would tell you what other fields you needed. After each customer question write down the fields that you need to get the answer to the question.

9 Make sure you have corrected all the mistakes you noticed after verification. Print out a copy of the corrected database. Put this in your **Verification** section and write a few lines explaining how you have corrected these mistakes.

10 Now you must do a search using the results of a search you have already made. You can do this by searching on more than one field. Make sure that your customer questions (see Step 8 above) are about more than one field. An example is the question about *blue Nokias* (colour and make). Make sure that you have two or three questions like this. Write about this and include the printouts of all the results of your queries. Make sure you have written the search down on each of your printouts. In your **Searches** section write down a few lines on the searches you have used and include all your printouts.

11 When you created your database you should have included some validation routines. These check that you are typing in data which is sensible. You will need to show how you created your routine. You will also need to show what happens when you type in invalid data. Here is an example of a validation check and the error message which appears when you type in invalid data.

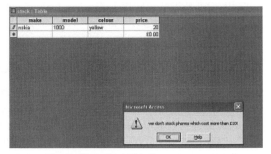

Screenshot of a validation error message
(20 has been entered into the price field)

Screenshot of a validation routine
(the price must be less than £10)

In the examples shown above the person creating the database thinks that the most expensive phone in this shop is £9.99. As a result she has included a validation routine which checks that the price is less than £10.

You need to write about your validation routines under the heading **Validation**. Make sure you have created at least two routines. Get printouts of the design of each one. Get printouts of the error messages which appeared when you typed in invalid data for each one. Write on each printout what it is about. Put these in your **Validation** section.

12 Now you must make some complex searches. This means that when you type in your query you must use the logical operators AND, OR and NOT. You must use at least two of these operators. On the phones database you could search for:

i) red or blue phones (colour = red OR blue)

II) Nokia phones which are less than £5 (make = Nokia **AND** cost < 5)

It is a good idea to show your query design screens for these complex searches.

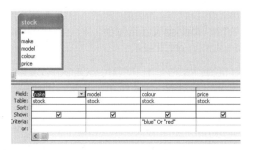

Design screen of query for blue or red phones

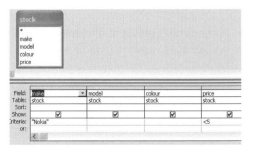

Design screen of query for Nokia phones less than £5

Print out screenshots of the designs of all your complex queries. Put these in your **Searches** section but make sure you write a few lines about each query saying what you are looking for. You must also say what you had to type in to get the right results.

13 You now need to say why you chose the software you used. The reasons you give must be because it was most suitable for the task. You must also write about other database software you could have used. You must say why your choice was better than the other software you could have used. These are three reasons you cannot use!

- It's the only one the school has got.
- It's the one you know the best.
- It's better than using a word processor or desktop publishing package.

You can compare it with a spreadsheet, providing the spreadsheet lets you search for data. The reasons you give must be about the data-handling features of the package. If your task is all about making searches then the reasons must be about how easy it is to search using your chosen software. If your task requires you to produce graphs then the reasons must be about how easy it is to produce graphs using your chosen software and so on. These reasons you give should be added to what you have written so far under the heading **Creation of the database**.

14 You will already have given your reasons for choosing the fields on your data capture form under the heading **Data collection and capture** (Step 8 above). Now you need to give reasons for choosing the field types and field lengths. This can be written about under the heading **Design of the database** (following on from Step 3 above). Many fields will be of a text type because letters of the alphabet or punctuation marks will be involved. You must explain this, however. Where you have used numeric field types you will need to say why the field had to be numeric. This could be because you will want to perform calculations or use some arithmetic functions on the data. You may want to use validation routines on numeric fields and logical/Boolean type fields. You must write about your choice of field type for every field. You must also write about your choice of field lengths. This is easiest done by using examples from your completed data capture forms. For each text field you could point out the longest item of data in that field. You will write that you must have a field length of at least that number of characters.

In order to gain a mark of 26 to 28 you will need to do all of 1 to 14 as well as the following. Some of the following advice may mean that you have to go back and change some of the write-up you have already done.

15 You must now make a list of your required outputs. In Step 1 above you were advised that one of the approaches to this work was to make a list of the searches you might have to perform on your database. The example was to make a list of customer queries. It is essential, if you want a mark greater than 25, that you have a list of searches in your **Introduction**. You need to explain that the results of these searches are your required output. You must also describe the nature of the required output. You will need to produce different types of report as well as graphs to gain a mark in this range. It is important that you list the forms of output the solution to your problem will need.

One part of your required output might be the results of performing a search for all the blue phones. You need to say if the output for this search will be in the form of a table or a report. You need to do this for all your queries. You must also describe any graphs or charts that you need to produce. You may have to produce graphs showing the most popular colour of phones. This will involve showing a graph of how many makes and model of phones come in red, blue, green and so on. If you use a bar chart then the colour with the highest bar will show the most popular colour.

16 In addition to what you have done for Step 8, you just need to say how the fields on your data capture sheet have enabled you to collect the data which will provide the required output. Remember this goes under the **Data collection and capture** heading.

17 You now need to explain how you considered the required output before making your final choice of field types and field lengths. Certain field types might be more appropriate than others when considering the required output. A Boolean/logical type might be appropriate in order to make sure that data entry is more accurate. On the other hand if the required output is a list of features of a mobile phone it might be better to use a text field containing the words 'yes' and 'no'. The use of a tick box approach might lead to squeezing too many fields on to the report and confusing the reader. As long as you can provide a plausible reason you will gain credit for your choices. This part of the write-up goes immediately after what you have already written under the heading **Design of the database**.

18 As well as what you wrote for Step 13 above, you now need to write about how your choice of software is capable of producing the type and form of output you wrote about in 15. Your solution will probably need to include different types of report and graphs. You will need to explain how the software you have chosen is the best for this. Put this under your heading **Creation of the database**.

19 Now you need to say how easy it was to use the software to:

- search for the records you needed for your required output;
- produce the required output formats i.e. reports, tables and graphs.

The best way of doing this is to write a User Guide. A user guide is a step by step description of how to use the software to make queries, reports and graphs. For each step you will write about how easy it is to use the software. This part of the write-up goes after what you have written so far under the heading **Creation of the database**. You will need to use screenshots to illustrate your guide. Here is an example of part of a user guide:

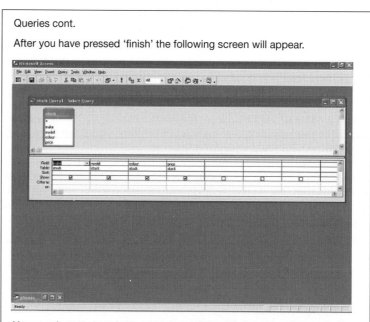

Queries cont.

After you have pressed 'finish' the following screen will appear.

Now you have to type in the search conditions that you are going to use. If you want to find all the blue phones you need to move the mouse pointer so it points at colour. Next you move the pointer down so that it is the fifth row (the one called Criteria). Now you click the left hand button of the mouse so that the caret appears. Type in the

Each part of the guide will describe how to use a software feature such as queries, reports, sorting, etc. After each description of a feature in the guide you should comment upon how easy it was to use that feature.

Here is a project which achieved a mark of 25. Not all of the project is included. There is one search on page 6 but the other searches (including complex searches) which are on pages 9 to 13 have been left out. Only one validation routine is shown here although the boy who did the project created another two on pages 7, 8. Remember that a minimum of two validation routines must be created. Some of the reasons for choice of software are also omitted. The candidate also explained about typing in new cars and how the people typing in the details are not used to databases. He gives the benefits of using input forms although acknowledging that in Excel you can hide columns and rows to make it look like an input form. Here is a list of the criteria for 23 to 25 marks and where they were met in the project.

Develop a method of collecting data.	Pages 1–3
Collect a range of data.	Pages 2, 3
Create a database using selected pieces of this data.	Pages 1, 4, 5
Give reasons for the choice of fields, field types and lengths	Pages 1, 4
Visually check the database for accuracy.	Page 5
Check the database for accuracy using validation routines	Pages 6–7
Edit the database in light of the mistakes found	Page 5
Using more than one condition, search the database for answers to specific questions.	Specific questions on page 1 and Searches on pages 6 and 9–13
Give reasons for the choice of software.	Page 5

The project could not achieve a higher mark as the required output is not in sufficient detail. A list of customer queries (page 1) would count as part of the required output. The form of the required output such as reports and graphs has not been described. A relational database might be needed where you would add on a table of the number of sales of the different makes. You would do this because of graphs of sales being required and different reports being needed. All the necessary criteria could be met by changing the reasons for each choice that was made. These choices would now relate to both the main stock file as well as the sales trends file.

Car database

■ Introduction

Mann's Autos is a company which sells second hand cars. At the moment they only use their computer to type out letters to send their customers. They don't use the computer for anything else in their showroom. They use a filing cabinet to keep all their records about the cars they sell. I am going to create a database to help the salesmen and the manager.

Before I create it I have to plan it and think about how to do it. Firstly I'll have to think about the fields so that they are suitable for the most popular queries. I'll have to find out some of the questions that customers ask. I'll ask the employees at the showroom.

When I asked the salesmen they told me that these were the most popular questions:

1 Have you got any blue cars?
2 Have you any Vauxhall Vectras?
3 I only have £5,000. Do you have any Fords that I can afford?
4 I need a car less than 2 years old or if it's not less than 2 years old it has to have less than 20,000 miles on the clock.
5 Have you any 4-door saloon cars for less than £9,000?
6 I need a car which has an engine size of at least 1.6 litres.
7 The car must have air-conditioning and driver and passenger airbags.

Question 1 tells me that I need the Colour of the car in my database.

Question 2 tells me that I need the Make and Model of the car in my database.

Question 3 tells me that I need the Price and Make of the car in my database.

Question 4 tells me that I need the Year the car was made and the Mileage of the car in my database.

Question 5 tells me that I need the Number of doors and Price of the car in my database.

Question 6 tells me that I need the Engine size of the car in my database.

Question 7 tells me that I need to have if the car has Air-conditioning and Airbags in my database.

This means I need these fields on my database.

Colour, Make, Model, Price, Year made, Mileage, Number of doors, Engine size, Air-conditioning and Airbags.

■ Data Capture and Collection

The next thing I had to do was collect information about cars for my database. I created a data capture form for 30 cars, after I had decided on the different fields. I used all the headings I got from the questions on my data capture form.

I collected lots of information about cars from Auto Trader and the Internet from www.autobytel.co.uk. On the autobytel site I searched for all the cars for less than £10,000. It gave me a list like this:

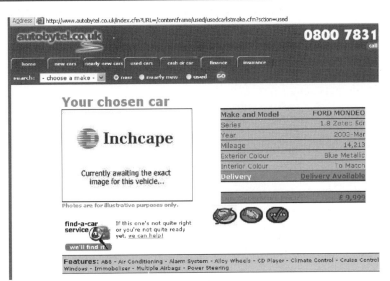

This gave me all the information I needed except for air-conditioning and airbags. If you click 🔘 next to the car it tells you about the air-conditioning and airbags in the Features box.

Overleaf is a page I used from Auto Trader. I only used the cars which had simple colours like red, blue and silver. I didn't use cars which had colours like Reflex blue, Desert beige and Red, Black roof. I didn't use blue metallic I just wrote it as blue.

I only used some of the information. Below you can see my filled in data capture forms.

I made sure I used data which had different prices, colours, numbers of doors and engine sizes.

Colour	Make	Model	Price	Year made	Mileage	Number of doors	Engine size	Air conditioning	Air bags
Silver	Peugeot	307	£5,995	2001	27,000	3	1.4	No	Twin
Silver	Peugeot	406	£3,200	1996	28,000	4	2.0	No	No
Burgundy	Renault	Clio	£2,795	1998	59,000	3	1.2	No	No
Red	Renault	Clio	£1,295	1998	45,000	3	1.2	No	No
Green	Renault	Clio	£3,895	2000	20,000	3	1.2	No	Twin
Red	Citroen	Saxo	£2,779	1999	31,765	3	1.0	No	No
Silver	Vauxhall	Astra	£3,025	1998	51,089	5	1.6	Yes	Drivers
Red	Peugeot	106	£3,299	1999	49,206	3	1.1	No	No
Blue	Renault	Laguna	£3,495	1998	52,469	5	1.8	Yes	Twin
Red	Toyota	Avensis	£3,495	1998	51,894	5	1.8	No	No
Blue	Ford	Fiesta	£3,528	1998	40,171	3	1.2	No	Drivers
Silver	Toyota	Corolla	£3,795	1998	63,011	5	1.3	No	No
Gold	Rover	25	£4,199	2000	55,891	3	1.6	No	Drivers
Red	Fiat	Punto	£4,199	2001	21,255	3	1.2	No	Twin
Blue	Citroen	Xantia	£4,699	1998	44,369	5	1.9	Yes	Twin
Silver	Mazda	Premacy	£5,199	1999	65,370	5	1.8	Yes	Drivers
Silver	Nissan	Almera	£5,399	2001	12,416	3	1.5	No	Drivers
Red	Toyota	Yaris	£5,439	2002	10,363	5	1.0	No	Drivers
Blue	Peugeot	406	£5,795	1999	26,000	4	1.8	Yes	Twin
Black	Smart	City	£6,000	2002	4,975	2	0.7	No	Twin
Green	Vauxhall	Corsa	£6,499	2003	13,234	5	1.2	No	Drivers
Grey	Vauxhall	Vectra	£6,695	2000	51,242	5	1.8	Yes	Twin
Silver	Ford	Focus	£6,750	2001	21,488	5	1.6	Yes	Twin
Blue	Honda	Accord	£6,995	1998	77,250	2	3.0	No	No
Silver	Rover	45	£6,995	2001	53,997	4	2.0	Yes	Drivers
Green	Volkswagen	Golf	£7,000	1998	56,007	5	1.6	No	Twin
Silver	Ford	Fiesta	£7,180	2003	6,683	5	1.4	Yes	Drivers
Red	Ford	Focus	£7,199	2000	46,347	5	2.0	Yes	Drivers
Silver	Toyota	Picnic	£7,295	1998	61,113	5	2.0	No	No
Red	Renault	Megane	£7,595	2000	26,556	5	1.6	Yes	Twin
Silver	Volvo	V40	£7,899	1999	61,150	5	2.0	No	No
Red	Mazda	MX-5	£8,199	2000	58,904	2	1.6	Yes	Drivers
Silver	Nissan	Almera	£8,299	2001	27,385	5	1.8	Yes	Twin
Silver	Ford	Focus	£8,595	2003	14,404	3	1.6	Yes	Drivers
Blue	Toyota	Avensis	£9,199	2002	21,002	5	2.0	Yes	Twin
Gold	Honda	CR-V	£9,499	1999	60,315	5	2.0	Yes	Twin
Silver	Ford	Mondeo	£9,999	2003	13,505	5	1.8	Yes	Drivers
Black	Volkswagen	Bora	£9,999	2003	13,700	4	1.6	Yes	Drivers

■ Design of the database

The next thing I did was to draw a table showing all the fields I was going to have in my database.

Field name	Field type	Field size	Validation check	Example
Colour	Text	10		Burgundy
Make	Text	12		Renault
Model	Text	8		Megane
Price	Currency		<10000	£9050
Year made	Number	Integer		1998
Mileage	Number	Integer	<100000	56789
Doors	Number	Integer	>1, <6	4
Engine size	Number	Decimal		1.6
Air conditioning	Logical/Boolean	1		y
Air bags	Text	8		drivers

I put in some validation checks:

• The price of a car must be less than £10,000.
• The mileage on the car must be less than 100,000
• The number of doors must be more than 1 and less than 6.

For each field, I looked at the data I had collected on my data capture form and chose the appropriate type. The Colour, Make and Model were made up of words and numbers so text seemed best. The price was a number with a £ sign so currency seemed the best. Year made, Mileage, Doors and Engine size had no text in them so I chose number. Air-conditioning had the answers yes or no so I chose Boolean. Airbags only had three answers so I chose text but I would use a drop down list when I made the database.

For the lengths of the fields I looked at the longest piece of data in each field and added one or two on for the text fields. The longest Colour was Burgundy (8) so I made it 10. The longest Make was Volkswagen (10) so I made it 12. Model had three records with a length of 7 so I made it 8. The longest value for Airbags was 'drivers' (7) so I made it 8.

■ Creation of the database

I used Microsoft Access to create my database. I created my table in Design view. I typed in each field name, then the data type and then the description. Here it is.

(4)

I chose Access because it is the best data handling package for my task. My task is to create a database which will make it easier for car salesmen to answer customer questions. That is its only use. If I had to make some graphs then Excel would have been a better choice. A lot of cars are sold every day and new cars come in to the showroom but the customer questions will tend to be the same. Access automatically saves your queries and it doesn't make any difference how many records you delete or add, the queries will still give you the right answer. With Excel you would have to type in your filters every time you wanted to answer a question even if you'd done it before.

■ Verification

Below you can see a printout of the database. I have highlighted the mistakes I made. I found these by looking at my data capture form to see what I should have typed in. These are the mistakes I had made:

Record No.	Mistake
7	1.8 instead of 1.6 for Engine size
10	Avenses instead of Avensis
15	drivers instead of twin airbags
18	2001 instead of 2002 year made
18	12416 instead of 10363 Mileage
18	yes instead of no for air-conditioning
19	Peogeot instead of Peugeot
22	Green instead of Grey
34	14444 instead of 14404

Here you can see my database before and after I had corrected my mistakes.

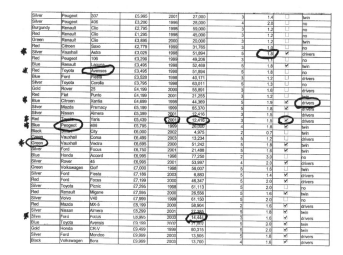

Before correction:

Colour	Make	Model	Price	Year made	Mileage	Number of doors	Engine size	Air conditioning	Air bags
Silver	Peugeot	307	£5,995	2001	27,000	3	1.4	☐	twin
Silver	Peugeot	406	£3,200	1996	28,000	4	2.0	☐	no
Burgundy	Renault	Clio	£2,795	1998	59,000	3	1.2	☐	no
Red	Renault	Clio	£1,295	1998	45,000	3	1.2	☐	no
Green	Renault	Clio	£3,895	2000	20,000	3	1.2	☐	twin
Red	Citroen	Saxo	£2,779	1999	31,765	3	1.0	☐	no
Silver	Vauxhall	Astra	£3,025	1998	51,894	5	1.8	☑	drivers
Red	Peugeot	106	£3,299	1999	49,206	3	1.1	☐	no
Blue	Renault	Laguna	£3,495	1998	52,469	5	1.8	☑	twin
Red	Toyota	Avenses	£3,495	1998	51,894	5	1.8	☐	no
Blue	Ford	Fiesta	£3,528	1998	40,171	3	1.2	☐	drivers
Silver	Toyota	Corolla	£3,795	1998	63,011	3	1.3	☐	twin
Gold	Rover	25	£4,199	2000	55,891	3	1.6	☐	drivers
Red	Fiat	Punto	£4,199	2001	21,255	3	1.2	☐	twin
Blue	Citroen	Xantia	£4,699	1998	44,369	5	1.9	☑	drivers
Silver	Mazda	Premacy	£5,199	1999	65,370	5	1.8	☑	drivers
Silver	Nissan	Almera	£5,399	2001	12,416	3	1.5	☐	drivers
Red	Toyota	Yaris	£5,439	2001	12,416	3	1.5	☑	drivers
Blue	Peogeot	406	£5,795	1999	26,000	4	1.8	☑	twin
Black	Smart	City	£6,000	2002	4,975	2	0.7	☐	twin
Green	Vauxhall	Corsa	£6,499	2003	13,234	5	1.2	☐	twin
Green	Vauxhall	Vectra	£6,695	2000	51,242	5	1.8	☑	twin
Silver	Ford	Focus	£6,750	2001	21,488	5	1.6	☑	twin
Blue	Honda	Accord	£6,995	1998	77,250	2	3.0	☐	no
Silver	Rover	45	£6,995	2001	53,997	4	2.0	☑	drivers
Green	Volkswagen	Golf	£7,000	1998	56,007	5	1.6	☐	twin
Silver	Ford	Fiesta	£7,186	2003	6,883	5	1.4	☑	drivers
Red	Ford	Focus	£7,199	2000	46,347	5	2.0	☑	drivers
Silver	Toyota	Picnic	£7,295	1998	61,113	5	2.0	☐	no
Red	Renault	Migane	£7,595	2000	26,556	5	1.6	☑	no
Silver	Volvo	V40	£7,999	1999	61,150	5	2.0	☐	no
Red	Mazda	MX-5	£8,199	2000	58,904	2	1.6	☑	drivers
Silver	Nissan	Almera	£8,299	2001	27,385	5	1.8	☑	twin
Silver	Ford	Focus	£8,995	2003	14,444	3	1.6	☑	drivers
Blue	Toyota	Avensis	£9,199	2002	21,002	5	2.0	☑	twin
Gold	Honda	CR-V	£9,499	1999	60,315	5	2.0	☑	twin
Silver	Ford	Mondeo	£9,999	2003	13,505	5	1.8	☑	drivers
Black	Volkswagen	Bora	£9,999	2003	13,700	4	1.6	☑	drivers

After correction:

Colour	Make	Model	Price	Year made	Mileage	Number of doors	Engine size	Air conditioning	Air bags
Silver	Peugeot	307	£5,995	2001	27,000	3	1.4	☐	twin
Silver	Peugeot	406	£3,200	1996	28,000	4	2.0	☐	no
Burgundy	Renault	Clio	£2,795	1998	59,000	3	1.2	☐	no
Red	Renault	Clio	£1,295	1998	45,000	3	1.2	☐	no
Green	Renault	Clio	£3,895	2000	20,000	3	1.2	☐	twin
Red	Citroen	Saxo	£2,779	1999	31,765	3	1.0	☐	no
Silver	Vauxhall	Astra	£3,025	1998	51,894	5	1.6	☑	drivers
Red	Peugeot	106	£3,299	1999	49,206	3	1.1	☐	no
Blue	Renault	Laguna	£3,495	1998	52,469	5	1.8	☑	twin
Red	Toyota	Avensis	£3,495	1998	51,894	5	1.8	☐	no
Blue	Ford	Fiesta	£3,528	1998	40,171	3	1.2	☐	drivers
Silver	Toyota	Corolla	£3,795	1998	63,011	3	1.3	☐	twin
Gold	Rover	25	£4,199	2000	55,891	3	1.6	☐	drivers
Red	Fiat	Punto	£4,199	2001	21,255	3	1.2	☐	twin
Blue	Citroen	Xantia	£4,699	1998	44,369	5	1.9	☑	twin
Silver	Mazda	Premacy	£5,199	1999	65,370	5	1.8	☑	drivers
Silver	Nissan	Almera	£5,399	2001	12,416	3	1.5	☐	drivers
Red	Toyota	Yaris	£5,439	2002	10,363	3	1.5	☐	drivers
Blue	Peugeot	406	£5,795	1999	26,000	4	1.8	☑	twin
Black	Smart	City	£6,000	2002	4,975	2	0.7	☐	twin
Green	Vauxhall	Corsa	£6,499	2003	13,234	5	1.2	☐	twin
Grey	Vauxhall	Vectra	£6,695	2000	51,242	5	1.8	☑	twin
Silver	Ford	Focus	£6,750	2001	21,488	5	1.6	☑	twin
Blue	Honda	Accord	£6,995	1998	77,250	2	3.0	☐	no
Silver	Rover	45	£6,995	2001	53,997	4	2.0	☑	drivers
Green	Volkswagen	Golf	£7,000	1998	56,007	5	1.6	☐	twin
Silver	Ford	Fiesta	£7,186	2003	6,883	5	1.4	☑	drivers
Red	Ford	Focus	£7,199	2000	46,347	5	2.0	☑	drivers
Silver	Toyota	Picnic	£7,295	1998	61,113	5	2.0	☐	no
Red	Renault	Migane	£7,595	2000	26,556	5	1.6	☑	no
Silver	Volvo	V40	£7,999	1999	61,150	5	2.0	☐	no
Red	Mazda	MX-5	£8,199	2000	58,904	2	1.6	☑	drivers
Silver	Nissan	Almera	£8,299	2001	27,385	5	1.8	☑	twin
Silver	Ford	Focus	£8,995	2003	14,404	3	1.6	☑	drivers
Blue	Toyota	Avensis	£9,199	2002	21,002	5	2.0	☑	twin
Gold	Honda	CR-V	£9,499	1999	60,315	5	2.0	☑	twin
Silver	Ford	Mondeo	£9,999	2003	13,505	5	1.8	☑	drivers
Black	Volkswagen	Bora	£9,999	2003	13,700	4	1.6	☑	drivers

■ Searches

In my introduction (page 1) I made a list of seven questions that customers might ask.

On the following pages you can see the queries I created and the printouts of the matching records.

1 Query design for Colour = blue

Printout of matching records

Colour	Make	Model	Price	Year made	Mileage	Number of doors	Engine size	Air conditionin	Air bags
Blue	Renault	Laguna	£3,495	1998	52,469	5	1.8	✔	twin
Blue	Ford	Fiesta	£3,528	1998	40,171	3	1.2	☐	drivers
Blue	Citroen	Xantia	£4,699	1998	44,369	5	1.9	✔	twin
Blue	Peugeot	406	£5,795	1999	26,000	4	1.8	✔	twin
Blue	Honda	Accord	£6,995	1998	77,250	2	3.0	☐	no
Blue	Toyota	Avensis	£9,199	2002	21,002	5	2.0	✔	twin

■ Validation

On the next few pages you can see the validation routines I wrote and screenshots showing that they worked.

This shows the design of my validation routine for the Price field:

This shows what happened when I typed in £30,025 by mistake:

Price	Year made	Mileage	Number of doors ▲
£5,995	2001	27,000	3
£3,200	1996	28,000	4
£2,795	1998	59,000	3
£1,295	1998	45,000	3
£3,895	2000	20,000	3
£2,770	1999	31,765	3
£30,025	1998	51,894	5
£3,299	1999	49,206	3
£3,495	1998	52,469	5
£3,495	1998	51,894	5
£3,528	1998	40,171	5

Microsoft Access

⚠ All cars must be less than £10,000

OK   Help

£5,439	2002	10,363	3
£5,795	1999	26,000	4
£6,000	2002	4,975	

In the data-handling strand you have to create your own database to gain a mark of 10 or more. In the three remaining strands you do not have to create your own work unless you want to achieve a mark of 20 or more. This means that, in modelling, control and measuring, if your teacher thinks you can achieve a high mark they can let you miss out the first 7 mark boxes. This may not be such a good idea, however, because if you fail to meet all the criteria for the 20–22 mark range, you will get zero. If, on the other hand, you do all the mark ranges up to 20–22 and fail to meet all the criteria you could still get a mark of 19. Your teacher will advise you on this.

Modelling can be divided into three ranges of marks: 0–13, 14–19 and 20–28. Again, your teacher will decide if it is more sensible for you to start working at the 14–19 mark range or even the 20–28 mark range rather than do all the mark ranges. This chapter will look at these three mark ranges and give guidance on how to achieve the criteria.

Here is the list of things you have to do to meet the first **five** mark boxes (13 marks):

1 Write about the workings of a model which you have used.

   Doing this will give you a mark of 2 if you have done it correctly.

2 Write about how you have used the different options available within the model.

   Doing numbers 1 and 2 correctly will give you a mark of 4. Your teacher may give you only 3 marks if you have done them both but not particularly well.

3 Write about how you have used a model to make decisions. Write about the consequences of these decisions.

   Doing **all** of numbers 1–3 correctly will give you a mark of 7. Your teacher may give you only 5 or 6 marks if you have done them all but not particularly well.

4 Use a model to discover the patterns within it. Understand how the model operates. Make simple predictions.

   Doing these three things correctly will give you a mark of 10. Your teacher may give you only 8 or 9 marks if you have done them but not particularly well.

5 Explore the effects of changing the data within the model. Make simple predictions about some of the effects of these changes.

   Doing numbers 4 and 5 correctly will give you a mark of 13. Your teacher may give you only 11 or 12 marks if you have done them all but not particularly well.

Here is a spreadsheet model called 'Sports shop'.

	A	B	C	D	E	F
1	Item	Number sold	Cost price	Selling price	Profit	Profit
2		per week			per item	per week
4	Kino trainers	124	£44.00	£49.99	£5.99	£742.76
5	Sadman trainers	99	£39.00	£43.99	£4.99	£494.01
6	Kino tracksuits	27	£24.50	£31.99	£7.49	£202.23
7	Sadman tracksuits	31	£22.00	£29.99	£7.99	£247.69
8	footballs	48	£5.00	£8.99	£3.99	£191.52
9	Goalagame boots	32	£22.00	£27.99	£5.99	£191.68
10	Nevermiss boots	41	£19.00	£24.99	£5.99	£245.59
11	shinpads	26	£14.00	£19.99	£5.99	£155.74
12	football shirts	132	£25.00	£49.99	£24.99	£3,298.68
13	football shorts	128	£12.00	£17.99	£5.99	£766.72
14	tennis rackets	12	£49.00	£69.99	£20.99	£251.88
15	tennis balls × 6	47	£15.00	£19.99	£4.99	£234.53
16	badminton rackets	15	£39.00	£44.99	£5.99	£89.85
17	shuttlecock tubes	47	£24.00	£29.99	£5.99	£281.53
18						
19				Total profit per week		£7,394.41

Here is a series of tasks for you to do so that you can achieve mark boxes 1–5. Each task corresponds to a mark range. Task 1 gives you mark range 1, task 2 gives you mark range 2 and so on. Your teacher should create the 'Sports shop' model so that you can use it to do these tasks.

Mark ranges 1–3 above do not have to be done to get a mark of more than 7. You only have to do 4 and 5. However, you are strongly advised to do all of 1–5 to get marks in the range 11–13.

TASK 1

Load the 'Sports shop' spreadsheet and print it out. On this printout write down what the spreadsheet is being used to calculate. Then write down which columns are used to do the calculations and write down which cells are used to calculate the number in F19.

TASK 2

Choose any row between row 4 and row 17. Change the number in column B. For example you could change the number B6. Write down which numbers changed in column F. Also, write about how they changed. In other words, if you increased the number in column B did the numbers in column F also increase or did they decrease?

TASK 3

Up to this point you could have produced just one printout. Now you need to have printouts showing the spreadsheet before and after you made changes. It is now going to be easier for you to write a separate report to go with your printouts. Before you change the numbers in the spreadsheet you need to write about what you are going to do.

For example, you could say that you are going to increase the profit on Kino trainers to a certain amount. You need to write down how you are going to change the selling price to do this. As well as printing out the original spreadsheet you need to print out the spreadsheet showing the new selling price and the new profit. If the cost price increases you need a printout to show the change to the profit.

You must do this for two or three changes. At least one must be an increase and there must be at least one decrease. Then you must write about what happened as a result. How much was the increase or decrease in profit?

TASK 4

This is similar to Task 3. You must write about what the spreadsheet does. You will write a report on your work using a word processor.

- You will change at least two variables in different columns.
- Make sure that increasing one of these variables makes another variable increase.
- Try and make sure that increasing a variable in a different column makes another variable decrease. Write about the effects of changing these variables.

Get a printout of each change you have made as well as a printout of the original spreadsheet.

In your report you will also need to write down some general rules about the spreadsheet. Here is the sort of thing you need to write. One rule could be:

increasing the variables in column ... causes an increase in column ... whereas increasing the variables in column ... decreases the values in column ...

As well as writing some general rules you must show that you fully understand how the spreadsheet works. Some of the columns contain formulas. You must write about the general effects of these formulae. The sort of thing you need to write is like this:

Column ... is the result of subtracting column ... from column ...

You need to do this for all the columns where there are calculations. You must also write down some predictions. You will write something like:

If I change the number in cell .... to 126 then I predict that the number in cell ... will go up to 376.

Whilst it would be acceptable to do two predictions it would be better if you made at least three predictions.

TASK 5

Now you will need to change several variables and the contents of a number of cells. You will need to increase the number and then decrease it.

● Before you make the changes you will need to make a prediction about what will happen when you change it. Write this in your report.
● You then print out the spreadsheet results to show if you were right or not.
● Write down in your report whether you were right or not.
● Number your printouts so that you can write down the number of each printout next to each prediction in your report. This will help your teacher mark your work.

You will need to do this for the increase and decrease of a number in one cell in column B, then column C and, finally, column D. This means that you will end up with six predictions together with six printouts.

In the next section you will learn about what a complex model is. This is because in order to get a mark of more than 13 you need to use a complex model.

> Complex models

A complex model is one that has at least six rows and six columns. It must use at least two operators (+, -, *, /). It must also have at least two of the features listed below:

1 A worksheet function. The use of =sum() is a simple formula and is not considered to be complex. Some examples of formulae that are appropriate include: average, if, count, countif, hlookup, vlookup, date, max, sumif, today and weekday.

2 The **appropriate** use of absolute cell references within a formula e.g. =A1/A2*B1

3 The use of conditional formatting e.g. negative values automatically appearing in red italics, positive numbers in black.

4 The use of cell and/or worksheet protection.

5 The use of validation checks.

6 The use of a macro.

7 A graph.

8 The use of filters as long as they are used as part of a whatif.

✔ **ADVICE**

The use of two worksheet functions will count as two features. This means that if you just use two different worksheet functions and two different operators and at least six columns and six rows this counts as a complex model.

Here is an example of a complex model:

	A	B	C	D	E	F	G	H	I	J
1	Item	Number sold	Cost price	Selling price	Profit	Profit	Stock at start	Stock at end	Re-order	Re-order
2		per week			per item	per week	of week	of week	level	yes/no
3										
4	Kino trainers	124	£44.00	£49.99	£5.99	£742.76	198	74	100	yes
5	Sadman trainers	99	£39.00	£43.99	£4.99	£494.01	186	87	100	yes
6	Kino tracksuits	27	£24.50	£31.99	£7.49	£202.2	88	61	75	yes
7	Sadman tracksuits	31	£22.00	£29.99	£7.99	£247.69	106	75	75	no
8	footballs	48	£5.00	£8.99	£3.99	£191.52	124	76	75	no
9	Goalagame boots	32	£22.00	£27.99	£5.99	£191.68	112	80	50	no
10	Nevermiss boots	41	£19.00	£24.99	£5.99	£245.59	101	60	75	yes
11	shinpads	26	£14.00	£19.99	£5.99	£155.74	88	62	50	no
12	football shirts	132	£25.00	£49.99	£24.99	£3,298.6	8 211	79	150	yes
13	football shorts	128	£12.00	£17.99	£5.99	£766.72	201	73	150	yes
14	tennis rackets	12	£49.00	£69.99	£20.99	£251.88	52	40	25	no
15	tennis balls × 6	47	£15.00	£19.99	£4.99	£234.53	121	74	100	yes
16	badminton rackets	5	£39.00	£44.99	£5.99	£89.85	56	41	25	no
17	shuttlecock tubes	47	£24.00	£29.99	£5.99	£281.53	152	105	75	no
18										
19				Total profit per week		£7,394.41				
20							number of items which need re-ordering			7

Here is the list of things you have to do to meet the next **two** mark boxes:

6 Use a complex model to discover the patterns within it; explore the effects of changing the data within the model; change the rules of the model; make simple predictions about some of the effects of these changes; write about how valid the model is.

Doing all of number 6 correctly will give you a mark of 16. Your teacher may give you only 14 or 15 marks if you have done them all but not particularly well.

7 Develop the model by changing the rules to solve a given task; write about how valid this model is in solving the task.

Doing all of numbers 6 and 7 correctly will give you a mark of 19. Your teacher may give you only 17 or 18 marks if you have done them all but not particularly well.

Here are tasks so that you can achieve mark boxes 6 and 7. Task 6 corresponds to mark range 6 and task 7 corresponds to mark range 7. Your teacher should create the new complex version of the 'Sports shop' model so that you can do these tasks.

TASK 6

If you have already done tasks 4 and 5 you won't have so much to do. However, you are now attempting to get marks which will get you at least a grade C for this piece of work. The following tasks are therefore more demanding. You must do tasks 4 and 5 for this new model. In addition you will need to change variables in columns G and I in the same way as you changed those in columns B, C and D in tasks 2 and 3 above. You need to make predictions and print out your results.

The first thing to do then is to repeat tasks 2 and 3 using the new model. Then you must change numbers in columns G and I and say what effect this has on column J. Remember to increase and decrease numbers.

The second thing to do is to repeat tasks 4 and 5 for this new model remembering to use columns G and I as well.

Your next task is to change some of the formulae. In the example above you could create a sale and reduce the selling prices by 10%. This would cause a change in the profit. You would need to change the formula in cell E4 to take this into account. The actual calculation would be profit = 90% of the selling price – cost price. You would need to change this into a formula. You would repeat this for every cell in column E.

You now need to make predictions about the effects of these changes on the profit per week for each item and the effect on the total profit per week. Print out the spreadsheet showing the changes in values and write down how accurate your predictions were.

Print out one copy of this spreadsheet showing the original formulae. Write on the printout what it is. Now print a copy showing the changed formulae. Highlight the changed formulae. Write on this printout what it is.

Now you need to write about how valid your model is. You need to describe a situation where this model could be used. In this example you could write about how a sports shop would use this model. You could write about what needs improving and what information and formulae would need to be added to make it more useful to the shop. You could actually make one of your suggested improvements for task 7.

TASK 7

In order to develop the model you need to add at least one more column. One possibility is to insert a column after column D. This new column E could be the new selling price if a sale is on. You could put a percentage in a cell such as B19 with the label in A19. The new selling price would be the old selling price (column D) reduced by the percentage in B19. You would now have to change the formula in column F (the old column E) to make sure it is the new selling price (column E) minus the cost price (column D).

You must now print out the spreadsheet showing the new formulae. Next you print it out showing the values.

You could now make some predictions on the effect of changing the percentage in B19. Print out the spreadsheet showing the results of your changes. Write about the predictions you made and the results of them.

Finally, you must write about the validity of the new model. You will say how much better than your previous version it is. You must still suggest further improvements to it and write about its shortcomings.

✔ A D V I C E

In order to get a mark higher than 19 out of 28 for this strand you will need to create your own model.

› Suggestions for modelling tasks

1 Design a spreadsheet showing the profits made by a sports shop. This will enable a shopkeeper to change numbers in stock, selling and cost prices to see how this affects re-ordering and total profits.

2 Design a spreadsheet showing the payroll of a company. This will allow the manager to change hourly rates, overtime rates and tax rates to see how this affects the total wage bill and the amount of money the company will have to pay the taxman.

3 Design a spreadsheet which will model the trajectory of a projectile. This will allow a user to change the values of velocity and angle of the projectile to determine distances travelled.

Your work will need to include:

- an explanation of why the model is needed and the uses it will be put to;
- research to determine the correct formulae;
- the design of a spreadsheet which shows the formulae and variables to be used;
- a report on the creation of the model;
- reasons why you chose the software you used;
- the results of experimenting with the model and the accuracy of predictions made;
- an evaluation of the model.

How to get started

The guidance given here is about the payroll task. You must use this as guidance to give you ideas and not just copy it out. That could lose you a lot of marks.

Setting out your work

You need to make your work easy for your teacher to mark and easy for the moderator to read. You will need to write up everything you have done. A good idea is to set out your work in different sections. The headings of each section are as follows:

- **Introduction:** You will need to write a couple of paragraphs explaining why the model is needed.

- **Design of the model:** Here describe and draw the structure of the spreadsheet you are going to create.

- **Creation of the model:** Here describe how you created your spreadsheet.

- **Predictions:** Here describe how you used your spreadsheet to test out your predictions or hypotheses.

- **Evaluation of the model:** Here write about how valid your model is when compared to what actually happens in the real world. You will also evaluate the software used.

 What you need to do to get the marks

1 When you have chosen your task, load a word processor on your computer and type in the details of the task you are going to do and why you think it is needed. You will describe the sort of situations that you think people could use your spreadsheet to model. In your write-up make a list of changes that you could make to the variables in the model. Type this under the heading **Introduction**.

In our example there will be variables such as rate of pay, overtime rates, hours worked, income tax and so on. You could describe how the model will tell you how much money each worker gets. You would need to go into some detail of exactly what information regarding the person's earnings the model would contain. You might say that the employer would type in the number of hours a person worked. The computer would calculate the wages for each person depending on the money they had earned and the tax they paid. The computer would be able to show the total wage bill and the total tax bill.

2 The next thing you will need to do is to put your thoughts onto paper. Using a pen or pencil you should sketch out some ideas. These will go into your **Design of the model** section. You should design the spreadsheet you are going to use. Design your model using a grid similar to the one below. You will need to include all the formulae you propose using. Here is a possible first design but you will produce two or three.

	A	B	C	D	E	F	G
1	Workers name	Hours worked	Rate of pay	Overtime	Weekly pay	Overtime pay	Total pay
2	J Sandhu	45	£6.35	=if(b2>35, b2-35, 0)	=(b2-d2)*c2	=d2*c2	=e2+f2
3	R Smith	30	£7.40				
4	M Ali	33	£6.85				
5							
6							

You will need to include income tax and tax allowances etc.

3 Load your spreadsheet software on to your computer and create your model. Use the details you put in your design table. You should have collected details about what you are typing in. You will need to include about 20 rows. Under the heading **Creation of the model** write a paragraph about *the reasons why* the software you have used is suitable for producing the model. All models have similar features so you should mention the fact that the software allows you to use features such as replication and automatic recalculation. Write about these and all the other features you had to use to create the model and how the software allowed you to do this. Your model must be complex so you will need to write about the features your software provides which allowed you to produce a complex model. You will also produce three or four printouts of the different stages of the creation of your model. Make sure these printouts contain formulae.

4 Now you need to do some predictions. Look at the uses you wrote down in your introduction. Some of the predictions might be:

- If J Sandhu's rate of pay is increased by £1 and R Smith's rate of pay is increased by 50p, I predict that there will be a total increase in the wage bill of £63.50.
- If the rate of income tax increased from 22% to 23% I predict that the total tax bill will rise by 5%.

Neither of these is likely to be true as the effect of income tax on the first one and the effect of higher rate tax in the second one has not been taken into account.

You must make a number of predictions. Make a prediction for each column in your spreadsheet which contains variables and about the effects of changing variables in any cell which you have used in absolute cell referencing. Write these down in your **Predictions** section.

You must then change the variables in the spreadsheet and print out the results. These printouts must go in the **Predictions** section. You must make a comment about each prediction. You could do this by writing your comments on the printouts. On every printout highlight the variable you have changed and the result of these changes.

5 Now write about the validity of the model. Make comments about whether you think the model would be useful to business. There may be certain things which have been left out which should have been included. This goes in your **Evaluation of the model** section.

To get a mark of between 23 and 25 you now need to do Step 6 below **as well as** what you have done for Step 1–5 above.

✔ A D V I C E

Doing all of numbers 1–5 correctly will give you a mark of 22. Your teacher may give you only 21 or 20 marks if you have done them all but not particularly well.

6 You now need to produce a step-by-step guide to how you used the software to create your model. You must include screen shots of each stage with examples of how you used each feature of the software. Show how you entered data, how you entered formulae, how you used replication. Show how you printed out your spreadsheet showing the values and how you printed out your spreadsheet showing the formulae. You will show how to print out the spreadsheet with gridlines showing and how you selected cell formats and increased or reduced row heights and column widths. This description will go immediately after what you wrote for 3, above, in your **Creation of the model** section.

To get a mark of between 26 and 28 you now need to do Step 7 below **as well as** what you have done for Steps 1–6 above.

7 You will now finish off your work by producing an evaluation of the software you used and how easy it was to create and use the model using this software. This will go in your **Evaluation of the model** section immediately after what you wrote for Step 5 above. Look at what you wrote for Step 6 above and say how easy, or otherwise, it was to use all the software features you used to create the model. You will also write about how easy it was to use the software features to change variables which you had to do in Step 4.

Here is a project which achieved a mark of 25. Not all of the project is included. There is a printout of the model on page 3 but the printout of the spreadsheet showing the formulae has been omitted to prevent plagiarism. If a student were to submit a project without a printout of the formulae the mark would be very low indeed.

Also omitted here are the printouts which the student used to show the spreadsheet being created column by column. The student had done this and had printouts to prove it.

Here is a list of the criteria for 23 to 25 marks and where they were met in the project.

It is a complex model because there are more than six rows and six columns. There are two operators: + in several cells and * in row 26. There is one worksheet function (IF) and absolute cell referencing in the grade column.

Design a complex computer model to provide the solution to a given task;	Pages 1, 2
Give reasons, related to the task, for choosing a piece of software for the solution;	Page 2
Use the software to construct the computer model;	Pages 2–5
Use the software to provide the answers required to solve the problem;	Pages 6, 7
Write about how valid this model is in solving the task;	Page 7
Write about how the model was created.	Pages 2–5

The project could not achieve a higher mark, as there is no evaluation of the software. The evaluation section could have had comments on how easy it was to use each feature mentioned in the creation of the model (pages 2–5). There should also be a comment on how easy it was to prove the validity for each of the predictions (pages 6, 7).

Teacher's mark book model

■ Introduction

Mrs Willets, my Science teacher, was complaining the other day that she was finding keeping her mark book up to date very difficult. I suggested keeping all her marks on a computer. I asked her to list the things she would like to do in her mark book. She wanted to keep the list simple so that I wouldn't find it too difficult to do. Here is her list:

- Have three grades for each test – pass, fail and commendation.

- Keep all her test results.

- Work out who had passed and who had failed.

- Have different pass marks and commendation marks for each test. The commendation mark will always be 1.6 times the pass mark.

- Have a total mark for all the tests and an overall pass mark and commendation mark.

- Be able to change any of the pass marks or commendation marks to see what difference it made to the number of passes and commendations.

- If there was one test to go she wanted to be able to work out what mark each pupil needed in the test to get a pass or commendation overall.

My spreadsheet will have just four test results, a total and 20 pupil records. There will be a formula to work out the grade for each pupil for each test. I will leave the fourth test result out so that Mrs Willets can experiment with the test results to see who will pass.

■ Design of the spreadsheet

Here was my first design (I used a word processor for my designs):

	A	B	C	D	E
1	Science Department mark book				
2	Pupil Name	Form	Gender	Test 1	Grade
3	Bloggs F	9A	M	85	=if(d3<50, "F",if(d3<80, "P","C"))
4	Sidhu J	9C	F	45	
5	Smith W	9C	M	31	
6	Khan I	9B	M	57	

I had put in columns for Name, Form, Gender, the result in the first test and the grade. I put the pass mark to 50 and the commendation mark to 80. IF(d3<50,'F', IF(d3<80,'P','C')) just means that if the number in d3 is less than 50 put the letter 'F' in cell E3. If it is not less than 50 but less than 80 put a 'P' in E3 otherwise put a 'C' in E3.

I soon realised that Mrs Willets was going to find it difficult to change the pass mark and commendation mark. I decided that I would put these marks in cells below the grade and change the formulae.

	A	B	C	D	E
1	Science Department mark book				
2	Pupil Name	Form	Gender	Test 1	Grade
3	Bloggs F	9A	M	85	=if(d3<50, "F",if(d3<80, "P","C"))
4	Sidhu J	9C	F	45	
5	Smith W	9C	M	31	
6	Khan I	9B	M	57	
7					
24					
25					50
26					=E25*1.6

Columns F to K were the same as D and E with the totals going in columns L and M.

F	G	H	I	J	K	L	M
Test 2	Grade	Test 3	Grade	Test 4	Grade	Total	Grade
52	=if(f3<E$25,	58	=if(h3<E$25,		=if(h3<E$25,	=D3+F3	=IF(L3<M$25,"F",
84	"F",if(f3<e$26,"P","C"))	86	"F",if(h3<e$26,'P','C'))		"F",if(h3<e$26,"P","C"))	+H3+J3	IF(L3<M$26,"P","C"))
63		69					
	55		45		50	=E25+G25+I25+K25	
	=g25*1.5		=i25*1.6		=k25*1.6	=E26+G26+I26+K26	

Row 25 would have the pass mark and row 26 would have the commendation mark, (pass mark × 1.6). Column L adds all the marks in Columns D, F, H and K together to get the total mark.

Creation of the model

After I had designed my spreadsheet I used Excel to create it. I used Excel because it had all the features I needed and let me solve all the problems I had. I needed to be able to make the columns the right width and the rows the right height. I also needed to have software which would let me type in a new pass mark and would automatically recalculate the new grade. Excel let me use the IF function. This means that depending on what one cell contains you can have different values in another. I wanted to be able to print out P, F or C depending on what the pupil's mark was. I also wanted to be able to type in a formula once and then copy it to a lot of other cells in the same column and Excel let me do this. It automatically changes the formula to add 1 to the row number. Excel lets me use absolute cell referencing which means that when I don't want the formula to add 1 on to the row number in the formula I just put a $ sign in it. This was useful when I used a cell to store the pass mark. On the next page you can see my spreadsheet. All I had to do to print it out was to go to File and then choose Print and then click on OK.

To printout the formulae I clicked on Tools, then Options, then Formulas and then OK.

Then I went to File and Print and OK.

Science Department mark book												
Pupil name	Form	Gender	Test 1	Grade	Test 2	Grade	Test 3	Grade	Test 4	Grade	Total	Grade
Bloggs F	9A	M	85	C	52	F	58	P		F	195	F
Sidju J	9C	F	45	F	84	P	86	C		F	215	P
Smith W	9C	M	31	F	63	P	69	P		F	163	F
Khan I	9B	M	57	P	68	P	56	P		F	181	F
Bibi F	9B	F	33	F	48	F	85	C		F	166	F
Mohammed A	9C	M	66	P	37	F	79	C		F	182	F
Evans K	9A	F	69	P	82	P	58	P		F	209	P
Hutton L	9B	F	73	P	55	P	56	P		F	184	F
Bhegal M	9A	F	60	P	83	P	35	F		F	178	F
Ali K	9B	M	59	P	53	F	33	F		F	145	F
Jones P	9C	M	45	F	60	P	49	P		F	154	F
Rowen P	9C	F	40	F	62	P	64	P		F	166	F
Lowe F	9A	M	83	C	48	F	71	P		F	202	P
Malhi R	9C	M	84	C	55	P	50	P		F	189	F
Dodd T	9B	F	74	P	52	F	77	C		F	293	P
Fryer A	9A	F	64	P	72	P	58	P		F	194	F
Cousins J	9A	F	39	F	44	F	58	P		F	141	F
Phillips L	9B	M	38	F	68	P	87	C		F	193	F
Powell C	9C	F	48	F	51	F	51	P		F	150	F
Grigg P	9A	F	39	F	64	P	72	C		F	175	F
				50		55		45		50		200
				80		88		72		80		320

③

Features I used in making my spreadsheet

The first thing I had to do to make my title and the pupils names fit in was to make the top row wider and merge cells. I clicked on row 1 and then clicked on Format, Row and then Height. I then typed in 28 and clicked on OK.

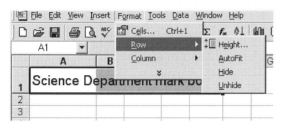

My heading was stretching from A1 to E1 and I didn't want any gridlines getting in the way of my heading so I highlighted A1 to A5 and went to Format, Cells, Alignment and clicked on Merge cells.

Next I typed in the headings Pupil name, Form, Gender, Test 1, Grade, Test 2, Grade, Test 3, Grade, Test 4, Total and Grade.

Pupil name	Form	Gender	Test 1	Grade	Test 2	Grade	Test 3	Grade	Test 4		Total	Grade

Next I clicked column B, went to Format then Column, then Width. I changed it to 5.

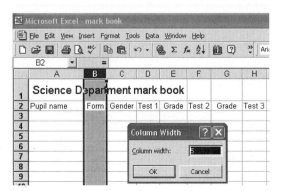

I changed column C to 7 and then changed all the other columns so that the contents fitted but so I could get them all on my printouts. Then I typed in the pupil names, the forms and genders and all the test marks.

Pupil name	Form	Gender	Test 1	Grade	Test 2	Grade	Test 3	Grade	Test 4	Grade	Total	Grade
Bloggs F	9A	M	85		52		58				195	
Sidhu J	9C	F	45		84		86				215	
Smith W	9C	M	31		63		69				163	
Khan I	9B	M	57		68		56				181	
Bibi F	9B	F	33		48		85				166	
Mohammed A	9C	M	66		37		79				182	
Evans K	9A	F	69		82		58				209	
Hutton L	9B	F	73		55		56				184	
Bhegal M	9A	F	60		83		35				178	
Ali K	9B	M	59		53		33				145	
Jones P	9C	M	45		60		49				154	
Rowen P	9C	F	40		62		64				166	
Lowe F	9A	M	83		48		71				202	
Malhi R	9C	M	84		55		50				189	
Dodd T	9B	F	74		52		77				203	
Fryer A	9A	F	64		72		58				194	
Cousins J	9A	F	39		44		58				141	
Phillips L	9B	M	38		68		87				193	
Powell C	9C	F	48		51		51				150	
Grigg P	9A	F	39		64		72				175	

I typed in my formulae like my design, making sure to put an = sign so I didn't get errors.

To save time I copied the formulae down so I typed =IF(D3<E$25,"F",IF (D3<E$26,"P","C")) into cell E3 and then clicked on E3 and went to Edit and Copy. Then I dragged it down to E22, went to Edit and Fill and Down.

I did that for all my formulae in columns G, I, K, L and M.

For the formulae in G26, I26, K26 and M26 I just copied cell E26 using Ctrl-C and pasted it one at a time into the other cells using Ctrl-V.

Predictions

After I had created my spreadsheet I made some predictions to test it.

1 If the mark to get a pass for test 1 was increased by 5 marks I predict that there will be the same number of pupils getting a pass but there would be 0 pupils getting a commendation.

2 If the mark to get a pass for test 2 was reduced by 5 marks I predict that there will be 4 more pupils getting a pass and 3 more pupils getting a commendation.

3 If the commendation mark was increased by 5 marks in test 3, the number of commendations would go down by 1.

4 I predict that J Cousins would need a mark of 59 for test 4 to pass the whole course.

Here are the printouts of my spreadsheet showing whether I was right for each one.

Science Department mark book				
Pupil name	Form	Gender	Test 1	Grade
Bloggs F	9A	M	85	P
Sidju J	9C	F	45	F
Smith W	9C	M	31	F
Khan I	9B	M	57	P
Bibi F	9B	F	33	F
Mohammed A	9C	M	66	P
Evans K	9A	F	69	P
Hutton L	9B	F	73	P
Bhegal M	9A	F	60	P
Ali K	9B	M	59	P
Jones P	9C	M	45	F
Rowen P	9C	F	40	F
Lowe F	9A	M	83	P
Malhi R	9C	M	84	P
Dodd T	9B	F	74	P
Fryer A	9A	F	64	P
Cousins J	9A	F	39	F
Phillips L	9B	M	38	F
Powell C	9C	F	48	F
Grigg P	9A	F	39	F
				55
				88

Science Department mark book						
Pupil name	Form	Gender	Test 1	Grade	Test 2	Grade
Bloggs F	9A	M	85	C	52	P
Sidju J	9C	F	45	F	84	C
Smith W	9C	M	31	F	63	P
Khan I	9B	M	57	P	68	P
Bibi F	9B	F	33	F	48	F
Mohammed A	9C	M	66	P	37	F
Evans K	9A	F	69	P	82	C
Hutton L	9B	F	73	P	55	P
Bhegal M	9A	F	60	P	83	C
Ali K	9B	M	59	P	53	P
Jones P	9C	M	45	F	60	P
Rowen P	9C	F	40	F	62	P
Lowe F	9A	M	83	P	48	F
Malhi R	9C	M	84	P	55	P
Dodd T	9B	F	74	P	52	P
Fryer A	9A	F	64	P	72	P
Cousins J	9A	F	39	F	44	F
Phillips L	9B	M	38	F	68	P
Powell C	9C	F	48	F	51	P
Grigg P	9A	F	39	F	64	P
					50	50
					80	80

1 I was wrong because I forgot that if there were 3 less pupils getting a commendation they would get a pass instead. There are 11 passes and 0 commendations.

2 I was wrong because I forgot that if there were 3 more pupils getting a commendation they would not be counted as passes any more. There are 13 passes and 3 commendations.

Science Department mark book				
Pupil name	Form	Gender	Test 3	Grade
Bloggs F	9A	M	58	P
Sidju J	9C	F	86	C
Smith W	9C	M	69	P
Khan I	9B	M	56	P
Bibi F	9B	F	85	C
Mohammed A	9C	M	79	C
Evans K	9A	F	58	P
Hutton L	9B	F	56	P
Bhegal M	9A	F	35	F
Ali K	9B	M	33	F
Jones P	9C	M	49	P
Rowen P	9C	F	64	P
Lowe F	9A	M	71	P
Malhi R	9C	M	50	P
Dodd T	9B	F	77	C
Fryer A	9A	F	58	P
Cousins J	9A	F	58	P
Phillips L	9B	M	87	C
Powell C	9C	F	51	P
Grigg P	9A	F	72	P
				45
				77

Science Department mark book						
Pupil name	Form	Gender	Test 4	Grade	Total	Grade
Bloggs F	9A	M		F	195	F
Sidju J	9C	F		F	215	P
Smith W	9C	M		F	163	F
Khan I	9B	M		F	181	F
Bibi F	9B	F		F	166	F
Mohammed A	9C	M		F	182	F
Evans K	9A	F		F	209	P
Hutton L	9B	F		F	184	F
Bhegal M	9A	F		F	178	F
Ali K	9B	M		F	145	F
Jones P	9C	M		F	154	F
Rowen P	9C	F		F	166	F
Lowe F	9A	M		F	202	P
Malhi R	9C	M		F	189	F
Dodd T	9B	F		F	203	P
Fryer A	9A	F		F	194	F
Cousins J	9A	F	59	P	200	P
Phillips L	9B	M		F	193	F
Powell C	9C	F		F	150	F
Grigg P	9A	F		F	175	F
					50	200
					80	320

3 This time I was right. The number of commendations went down from 6 to 5.

4 I was right again. As you can see a mark of 59 was enough to give J. Cousins a pass overall.

■ Evaluation of the model

I thought that on the whole the model worked well. A teacher could put in their own pupils' names and marks and pass mark. It would tell them who had passed, got a commendation or failed. Teachers could change the pass marks and commendation to suit themselves. I think it is easy to use.

I could make some improvements though. The spreadsheet doesn't show how many pupils had passed or got commendations. This could be done quite easily by putting in a formula using COUNTIF and could be done for every test and the total mark. This could be done in row 23 for passes and row 24 for commendations e.g. =COUNTIF(E3:E22,"P") for passes.

The other main problem is that at the moment all the tests have to be out of 100. It would be easier if there was an extra column between the test mark and the grade for each test. What the test was out of could be put in row 25. The mark out of 100 could be worked out by using a formula like =d3*100/d25.

Another improvement is that conditional formatting could be used to give each cell in the grade column a different colour like red for fail, green for pass and purple for commendation.

In the data-handling strand you have to create a database to gain a mark of 10 or more. However, in the three remaining strands you do not have to create your own work unless you want to achieve a mark of 20 or more. This means that, in modelling, control and measuring, if your teacher thinks you can achieve a high mark they can let you miss out the first 7 mark boxes. This may not be such a good idea, however, because if you fail to meet all the criteria for the 20–22 mark range, you will get zero. If, on the other hand, you do all the mark ranges up to 20–22 and fail to meet all the criteria you could still get a mark of 19. Your teacher will advise you on this.

Control can be divided into three ranges of marks: 0–13, 14–19 and 20–28. Again, your teacher will decide if it is more sensible for you to start working at the 14–19 mark range or the 20–28 mark range rather than do all the mark ranges. This chapter looks at these three mark ranges and gives guidance on how to achieve the criteria.

First of all we will look at what you must do to get up to 13 marks for this project. Here is the list of things you have to do to meet the first **five** mark boxes:

1 Write about how some everyday devices respond to signals and commands.

Doing this will give you a mark of 2 if you have done it correctly.

2 Specify an outcome. Write down how you controlled a screen turtle or robot to achieve this outcome.

Doing both these correctly will give you a mark of 4. Your teacher may give you only 3 marks if you have done them both but not particularly well.

3 Write down how you controlled a screen turtle or robot to achieve the specified outcome by a series of instructions. Write down the instructions used.

Doing numbers 2 and 3 correctly will give you a mark of 7. Your teacher may give you only 5 or 6 marks if you have done them all but not particularly well.

4 Save the instructions as a program. Print out the program. Annotate the program.

Doing 2, 3 and 4 correctly will give you a mark of 10. Your teacher may give you only 8 or 9 marks if you have done them but not particularly well.

5 Write about how you used precision in forming instructions. Write about how you used precision in sequencing instructions.

Doing numbers 2–5 correctly will give you a mark of 13. Your teacher may give you only 11 or 12 marks if you have done them all but not particularly well.

Here is a series of tasks for you to do so that you can achieve mark boxes 1–5.

TASK 1: Write down four examples of devices which use computer control. Say what is being controlled and write about what is being input to the device. Here is one example.

Device	What is being controlled	Input
Central heating	Water being pumped from the boiler to the heaters	Room temperature from a temperature sensor

TASK 2: You will use a programming language such as Logo. When you go on to the higher marks you will need to draw a complex shape like a house. For this task, however, you can just draw one window, one door and a roof. You must write a line or two saying what you are drawing.

Next, you must use the programming instructions to draw a picture of a window, a door and a roof. The window could be a little square and the door could be a rectangle. Write a few lines saying what you have drawn for your picture.

Use Logo to type in your instructions to control the screen turtle. Write about how you used Logo to make the drawing on the computer. Write down a few lines to say which instructions you used. You do not have to print out the instructions from the computer. You do need a printout of the window, door and roof from the computer.

TASK 3: On your printout of the shapes you created, you have to write down what instructions you used. If you had drawn a square window you would write on your shape like this:

Forward 50

right 90 ➝ Forward 50

Forward 50   Forward 50

Forward 50

You should either write down the instructions you used or get a computer printout of the instructions used like this:

```
? fd 50
? rt 90
? fd 50
? rt 90
```

Make sure you do this for all your shapes.

TASK 4: You now need to save the instructions as a program. You will have to write about how you saved it. If you are using Logo you will write: After I had typed in the instructions to draw my shapes I clicked on 'File' and clicked on 'Save Project As'.

The next part of the work would be to explain (with screenshots) how the file was saved.

Imagine

File   Edit   View   Options   Page   Help

New Project...

Open Project...   F3

Open Demo Project...   F11

Save Project   Shift+F2

Save Project As...   F2

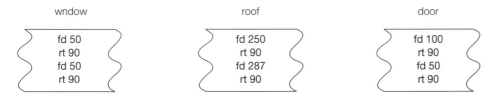

You need to print out the programs for each of your shapes. These are the starts of programs; you would have to print them all out.

wndow	roof	door
fd 50 rt 90 fd 50 rt 90	fd 250 rt 90 fd 287 rt 90	fd 100 rt 90 fd 50 rt 90

> **TASK 5:**   Now you need to write about what would have happened if you had typed in a wrong number. These are the starts of programs; you would have to print them all out.

For example, for the window, you could show what would have happened if you had typed in 100 instead of 90 like this:

You should show what would have happened if you had typed in a wrong instruction such as **backward** instead of **forward**.

You should know what would have happened if you had typed in the correct instructions but in the wrong order. This is the door with the lines drawn in the wrong order.

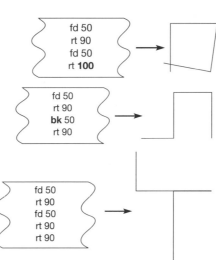

```
fd 50
rt 90
fd 50
rt 100
```

```
fd 50
rt 90
bk 50
rt 90
```

```
fd 50
rt 90
fd 50
rt 90
rt 90
```

> Complex patterns or shapes

In order to achieve either of the next two mark ranges you must produce complex patterns or shapes. You must do everything that you would do for 11–13 marks, but for the new complex patterns.

A complex pattern or shape can be one which combines shapes you may have already drawn separately. You are now going to combine them into a more complex shape.

The task which is being shown here is to draw a house using different programs. One to draw a window, one to draw a door, one to draw a roof and one to draw the walls.

You should have done tasks 2–5 above for the window, the door and the roof. Now you are going to combine them into one complex program.

Now we need to look at what you have to do to get a mark between 14 and 19 for this project. Here is the list of things you have to do to meet the next **two** mark boxes:

6 Write about how you tested and refined the program. Don't forget you must make sure you have done tasks 1–5 for the new combined program as well as for each part of the program. Each separate program you have written for tasks 1–5 will have to be written as a procedure in the new program.

7 Write about how you used efficiency and economy in framing instructions.

Here is a series of tasks for you to do so that you can achieve mark boxes 2 to 7.

✔ ADVICE

Doing all of 2–6 correctly (and don't forget you must have done tasks 1–5 for the new combined program as well as the parts of the program) will give you a mark of 16. Your teacher may give you only 14 or 15 marks if you have done them all but not particularly well.

✔ ADVICE

Doing all of 2–7 correctly will give you a mark of 19. Your teacher may give you only 17 or 18 marks if you have done them but not particularly well.

TASK 6: First of all, you must write a line or two describing the complex shape you are going to draw. It would be a good idea to make a hand drawn sketch of the shape. A couple of lines describing the house (for example), how many windows, the shape of the roof, one door or two, etc.

Here is an example of a sketch of a house. Notice that it does not have to be accurate, you are only trying to give the reader some idea of what it will look like.

You have already used programming instructions to draw a picture of a window, a door and a roof. The window should have been a little square and the door a rectangle. The roof is a trapezium.

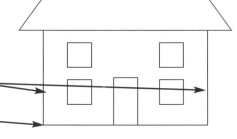

The next part of the task is to draw the walls and floor of the house in a program together with the roof, windows and door.

You will need to use procedures if you are to make this house.

You will need to define procedures for a roof, a window (window is a Logo command so you will need to call this procedure 'windo'), a door and a shell (the walls and floor). You will need to print out each procedure as well as the final program.

To windo	To roof	To door	To shell
repeat 4 [.......	home pu fd	repeat 2 [..........	home rt 90 ......
....	.....	....	....

You could use a procedure for the whole house e.g.

To house
door   windo   windo   etc.

....

When you run the whole program you will find that the shapes do not come out properly because of little mistakes you have made. You will need to annotate these mistakes and write about what caused them.

You will need to:

● print out your program showing the mistakes;
● write about where you typed in the wrong command;
● print out the resulting shape;
● write about how you put some commands in the wrong order;
● print out the shape showing how it came out all wrong;
● write about how you corrected the mistakes;
● print out the new version of the program.

Because you are showing, testing and refining you will need to show at least three stages in your development. This means three versions of the wrong house and three of the corrected program. Make sure that each corrected version is better than the previous version!

A printout of the development of the house might be:

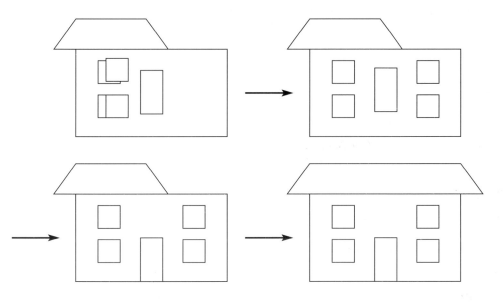

You would need to print out the programs for each stage and also point out which instructions were wrong and write about how you corrected them.

TASK 7: This should be fairly straightforward. You should have been using loops and procedures in Task 6. If you haven't, then you will need to re-write your program and define procedures as necessary.

All you should have to do now is to write on each procedure where you have used REPEAT loops. You must give examples of how the procedures would have looked had you not used loops. You will need to write about the advantages of using loops rather than repeating commands. This mark range is for grade B candidates and so you are expected to give appropriate reasons.

You must also write on your main program where you have used procedures and say why they are necessary. Again the reasons you give must be appropriate.

> ✔ **A D V I C E**
>
> In order to get a mark higher than 19 out of 28 for this strand you will need to create your own control system. It cannot be a virtual system. You must use physical sensors and real equipment.

> Suggestions for control system tasks

1 Create a greenhouse control system.

To include:
- a sensor to measure temperature;
- a sensor to measure light;
- a lamp to give out light;
- a fan to lower temperature;
- a heater to raise the temperature;
- documentation of the system.

2 Create a washing machine control system.

To include:
- a sensor to measure temperature;
- a sensor to measure water level;
- an inlet valve to let in water;
- a lock for the washing machine door;
- a heater to heat the water;
- documentation of the system.

✔ **ADVICE**

For the highest range of marks you will need to include feedback. You will also have to show where in your program it is and also explain how feedback works.

Your work will need to include:

- designs of the equipment and programs involved in the experiment;
- at least two different sensors;
- a write-up describing how you connected all the equipment to a computer;
- photographs showing the constructed equipment;
- how you used precision in forming instructions;
- a description of how the program developed including failures.

How to get started

The guidance given here is about the washing machine task. You must use this as guidance to give you ideas and not just copy it out. That could lose you a lot of marks.

Setting out your work

You need to make your work easy for your teacher to mark and easy for the moderator to read. You will need to write up everything you have done. A good idea is to set out your work in different sections. The headings of each section are as follows:

- **Introduction**: Here you need to write a paragraph about which experiment you are doing.

- **Design of the experiment**: In this section show sketches of the experiment you hope to carry out together with designs of the program.

- **Construction of the experiment**: You will describe how you put all the equipment together and describe the sensors you have used and what they were used to measure.

- **Development of the program**: describe how you tested and refined your program.

❯ What you need to do to get the marks

1 When you have chosen your task, load a word processor on your computer and type in the details of your planned experiment. You will describe all the things you hope your model of the washing machine will do. Type this under the heading **Introduction**.

In our example there will be inputs such as water level and temperature. There will be outputs such as signals to switch the water valve and heater on and off as well as motors to make the drum go round and signals to lock the door.

2 The next thing you will need to do is to put your thoughts onto paper. Using a pen or pencil you should sketch out the layout of the experiment. These will go into your **Design of the experiment** section. You should draw all the equipment you are going to use. You should also show the outline of the program you are going to write. Below are guides to how you would start this but these are incomplete. Obviously you would need to have a completed section to gain the marks.

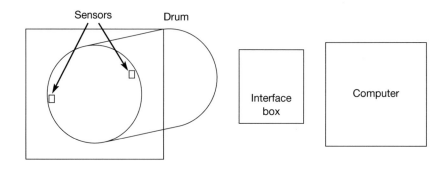

You would obviously do a much fuller diagram showing all the parts as well as the leads from the washing machine to the interface and from the interface to the computer. You will also need to include designs of the program. One of the procedures might look like this:

Temperature

Is the temperature less than 40 $\xrightarrow{\text{yes}}$ switch heater on

↓ no

switch heater off

You should do this for each procedure and the main program.

3 Now you need to create your experiment. You will need to write about how you set it up. Write about how the sensors were included in the equipment and about how they were connected to the interface box and write about how this was connected to the computer. Take some digital photographs of the experiment (at different stages) and insert them into your write-up. Put a line or two of writing next to each photograph and label the equipment. Put all this under the heading **Construction of the experiment**.

Load your control software on to your computer and write your programs. Use the outlines of the program you put in your design to guide you. You should print out your program and procedures showing how you made changes. You will have written procedures which don't work first time you try them. You will need to print these out and write on them where they went wrong. You will have made errors because statements were in the wrong order and you will have made errors because the values you typed in were wrong or missing. You will need to show printouts of procedures for both types of error. You will also need to show printouts of the corrected versions. Photos of the results on the experiment of incorrect sequencing and incorrect instructions should also be provided. You will also need to write on each procedure where you have used loops. You must give examples of how the procedures would have looked had you not used loops. You will need to write about the advantages of using loops rather than repeating commands. In addition, you will need to annotate your main program highlighting where you have used procedures and say why they are necessary. You will also need to print out a copy of your work directory or folder showing that you have saved the programs.

All this will need to go under the heading **Development of the program**.

To get a mark of between 23 and 25 you now need to do Step 4 below **as well as** what you have done for Steps 1 to 3 above.

4 You now need to give a detailed description of the sensors. You should write down the type of sensor being used and the variable it is measuring. You will then explain how it does this. For example, for a microprocessor-controlled oven, you would describe how an analogue temperature sensor works and that it transmits the current temperature of the oven via an interface to the microprocessor. You will need to describe the sensors in your washing machine in the same way.

5 Here, you will write about your choice of software. Immediately after the heading **Development of the program** write a paragraph about *the reasons why* the software you have used is suitable for creating the programs. Certain types of control software have similar features so you should mention the fact that the software allows you to use loops, procedures, labels for outputs, programming the interface box and so on. Write about these and all the other features you had to use to write your program and how the software allowed you to do this. Your device must be physical (not virtual) so you will need to write the features your software provides which allowed you to produce a physical system.

To get a mark of between 26 and 28 you now need to do Step 6 below **as well as** what you have done for Steps 1 to 5 above.

✔ **A D V I C E**

Doing *all* of numbers 1–3 correctly will give you a mark of 22. Your teacher may give you only 21 or 20 marks if you have done them all but not particularly well.

✔ **A D V I C E**

Doing *all* of numbers 1–5 correctly will give you a mark of 25. Your teacher may give you only 24 or 23 marks if you have done them all but not particularly well.

6 You must make sure that you have used feedback in your system. In the OCR specification it says:

A full explanation of how the output data is modified according to the data received from sensor(s) is required together with examples of how the output data modifies the input to the sensors.

This means that a system whose output does not affect the input is not acceptable. This means that your system will have to have feedback using analogue sensors. In your washing machine program you will need to write on your procedures for temperature and water level where exactly the feedback is taking place. You will need to explain what feedback is using the statement from the OCR specification as a guide. In addition, a paragraph will need to be included describing how you included feedback in the program, what it was used to control, and how it does control it. This will be the final part of your **Development of the program** section.

Here is a project which achieved a mark of 22. Not all of the project is included. There is one output screen on page 5 but the other one has been left out. There is one Motor screen on page 6 but the other two have been left out. These three screens would be needed in the final project. The descriptions of the many loops in the programs have also been omitted. These would need to be explained even though there are no repeat loops there are other loops. Some description is present (particularly for the temp < 23 loop) but some have been deliberately left out). The other omission is the description of wrong sequencing for the temperature element of the program. There were similar problems to those met with the light sequencing but these have been left out. They would have to be in place to merit the final mark awarded.

Here is a list of the criteria for 20 to 22 marks and where they were met in the project.

Design an experiment which uses control equipment to provide the solution to a given task	Page 1
Construct the experiment and use at least two different sensors	Page 2 onwards
Write about how they connected all the equipment to a computer	Pages 2–4
Provide diagrams or photographs showing the constructed equipment	Pages 2–4
Write about how they used precision in forming instructions	Pages 4–6
Write about how they used precision in sequencing instructions	Page 5
Write about how they used efficiency and economy in framing instructions	Page 7
Save the instructions as a program	Page 7
Write about how they trialled the program	Pages 4–7

The project could not achieve a higher mark as reasons for the choice of software have not been given. Here Logicator has been used; it is an excellent program and provided all the features needed. It is not within the remit of this book to say which is the best control software available but the candidate would be expected to do so in order to gain 25 marks.

To gain 28 marks, feedback would need to be included. This is quite simple to identify in this project as the roof being raised should lower the temperature and this in turn may require the ramrod to be lowered. The feedback is therefore present in the system and would only need to be identified in the programs and explained.

Greenhouse Control System

■ Introduction

The Biology department in school grows a lot of plants in their greenhouse. This is okay during term time and when the technicians are there and sometimes during the holidays. But often there is no one to look after the plants and so they have to be taken home by the teachers so that they don't die. I am going to create a computer-controlled model of a greenhouse and if it works it will help the Biology department make a real-life version so the plants don't have to be moved. Here are the things I want my system to do:

● If it is too dark switch a lamp on.
● If it is light switch it off.
● If it is too hot open a ventilator.
● If it is cool close the ventilator.

■ Design of the experiment

Here was my design of the experiment:

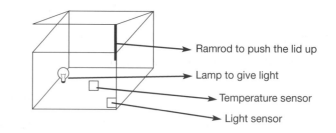

I am going to use wooden sticks for the frame of the greenhouse.

Here are the designs for my program

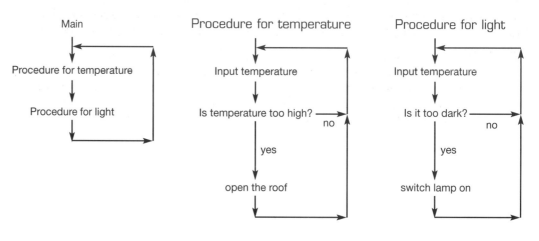

■ Construction of the experiment

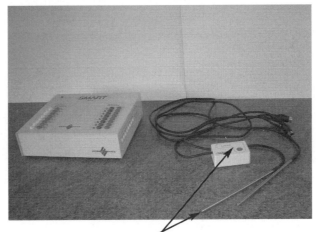

After I had designed my experiment I got some wood and nailed it together. I used see through plastic for the windows.

The next step was to get the interface box and sensors. Here is a light sensor and two temperature sensors next to the interface box.

The temperature sensor will transmit the temperature of the greenhouse in the form of a voltage which will be converted to a digital value by the interface so that the computer will understand it. The light sensor will transmit a voltage representing the amount of light and the interface box will convert this to a digital number for the computer. The temperature sensor is measuring how hot it is and if it is too hot the roof will open. The light sensor is measuring how cloudy it is and if it is very cloudy the light will come on.

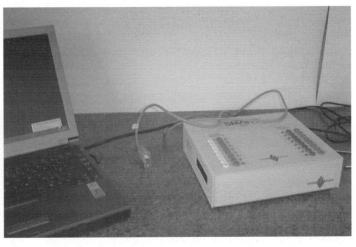

Here is the ramrod which I am going to use to raise the lid when it is too warm in the greenhouse.

Here is the lamp which will light up when it gets cloudy outside the greenhouse.

Here is the laptop I am going to use.

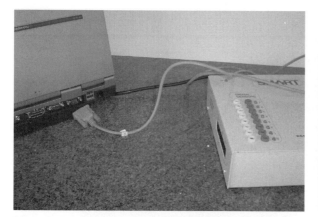

Here is where I plugged the interface box into the laptop.

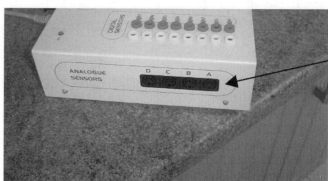

This is where you plug the sensors into the interface box.

Here is a photo of the light sensor connected to the interface box.

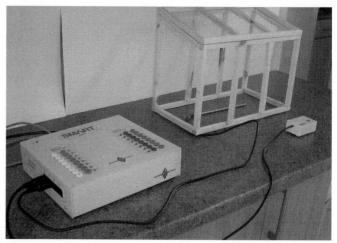

This is a photo of the temperature sensor and the light sensor connected to the interface box.

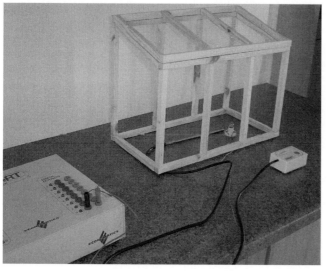

Here is a photograph of the lamp and the sensors. The light sensor is outside the greenhouse to detect the amount of daylight. If it went inside the greenhouse it would be affected by the lamp. The temperature sensor is inside the greenhouse.

Here is a photograph of the ramrod connected to the lid.

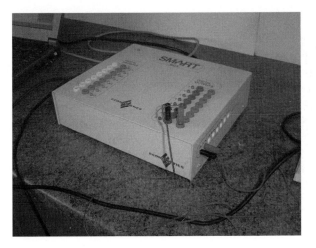

Here is a photograph of the interface box with all the leads connected.

Development of the program

The first thing I did was to write a program to control the light coming on.

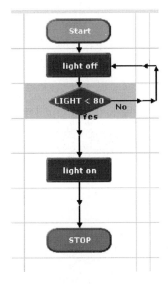

This was my first attempt but when I ran it the light came on even though it was still very light!

I had obviously got the number wrong.

This is an example of not being precise in forming instructions.

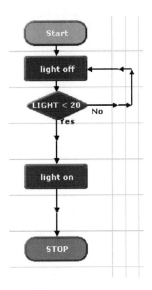

This was my second attempt but when I ran it the light stayed off even when it was getting really dark.

20 was obviously too low.

This is another example of not being precise in forming instructions.

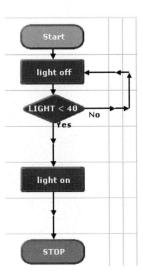

This was the value that seemed to work best. The light only came on when it started to get gloomy.

Here is the window showing the outputs setting for the light off instruction.

The problem I soon spotted was that the light would come on when it was night time but I didn't want that. I only wanted it to come on when it was gloomy during the daytime but to go off when it was night time. From the flowcharts, above, it seemed that 40 was the value at which I wanted the light to come on but 20 was dark so this is when it could switch off.

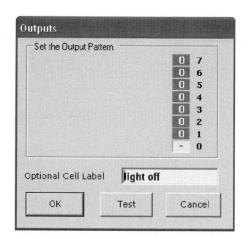

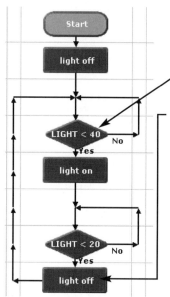

This program didn't work because the two decision boxes were in the wrong order. If the light value is less than 20 then the light keeps switching on and off. This is because if the light value was 15 then it is less than 40 so the light switches on.

If it is 15 it is also less than 20 so the light switches off and goes back to the LIGHT < 40 box.

This is an example of not being precise in sequencing instructions.

This time it worked fine because this program sees if the light value is less than 20 to begin with. If it is then it leaves the light switched off. If it isn't then it checks to see if it is less than 40 (this means it would be between 20 and 40). If it is between 20 and 40 the light comes on and it goes back to see if it has dropped below 20. If it isn't the light stays on and the program starts again.

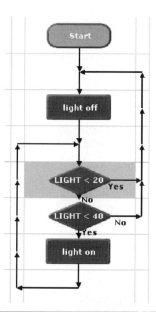

Here is the lamp on with the value between 20 and 40.

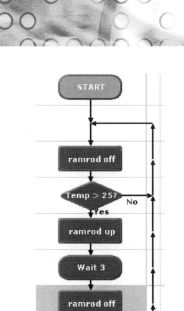

This was my final flowchart for the ramrod pushing the roof up if the temperature is above 25 and then switching the ramrod off.

If the temperature falls below 23 then the ramrod comes down. Here are the motor settings for the ramrod up.

This shows the ramrod working.

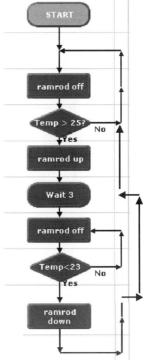

There is a problem. If the ramrod is up and the temperature is higher than 25 the ramrod will be pushed up even further!

This meant that I had to re-write the program.

This made sure that the ramrod only came down if it was already up. It also meant that while it was up the program only checked to see if the temperature was less than 23. This was because the loop only ends once the temperature is less than 23.

In order to save me having to put all the programs together into one long one I used procedures for them and then linked the procedures.

This is one procedure. It makes the light come on or off depending on the reading.

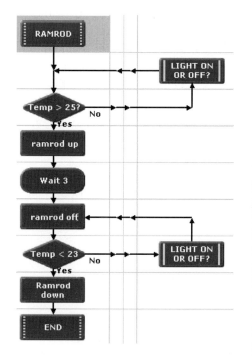

This procedure pushes the ramrod up if the temperature is higher than 25. If it isn't then it goes to the light procedure. Once the ramrod is up the procedure checks to see if the temperature is less than 23. The temperature is already above 25 and it may take a long time to cool down even with the roof open. The loop checking if it is less than 23 could be done several times. I have put a light check in because it might get cloudy but as long as the temperature stays higher than 25 the light could stay off. With the light check procedure here it makes sure this won't happen.

With these two procedures the whole program only has to be like the program on the left. This works fine and the greenhouse can now be light when it is cloudy and cool down when it is hot without any human interfering. Here is the proof that I saved these programs:

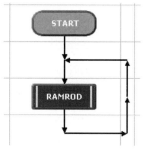

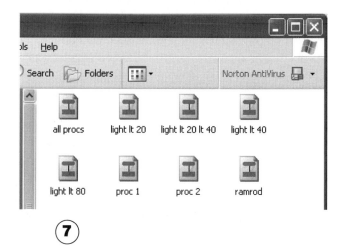

In the data-handling strand you have to create your own database to gain a mark of 10 or more. However, in the three remaining strands you do not have to create your own work unless you want to achieve a mark of 20 or more. This means that, in modelling, control and measuring, if your teacher thinks you can achieve a high mark they can let you miss out the first 7 mark boxes. This may not be such a good idea, however, because if you fail to meet all the criteria for the 20 to 22 mark range, you will get zero. If, on the other hand, you do all the mark ranges up to 20 to 22 and fail to meet all the criteria you could still get a mark of 19. Your teacher will advise you on this.

Measuring is simpler than control and modelling. There are only two ranges of marks which can be attempted. These are 0–19 and 20–28. Again, your teacher will decide if it is more sensible for you to start working at the 0–19 mark range or the 20–28 mark range rather than do all the mark ranges.

This chapter will look at the mark ranges and give guidance on how to achieve the criteria.

First of all we will look at what you must do to get up to 19 marks for this project. Here is the list of things you have to do to meet the first **seven** mark boxes:

1 Write about how everyday devices contain equipment which measure or monitor events.

   Doing this will give you a mark of 2 if you have done it correctly.

2 Give examples of everyday devices that contain equipment which measure or monitor events.

   Doing 1 and 2 correctly will give you a mark of 4. Your teacher may give you only 3 marks if you have done it but not particularly well.

3 Write about how you have connected computers to external devices that contain equipment which measure or monitor events.

   Doing *all* of numbers 1 to 3 correctly will give you a mark of 7. Your teacher may give you only 5 or 6 marks if you have done them all but not particularly well.

4 Provide printouts and explain how you got the computer to display the measurement results.

   Doing *all* of numbers 1 to 4 correctly will give you a mark of 10. Your teacher may give you only 8 or 9 marks if you have done them but not particularly well.

5 Explain the meaning of the displayed results.

   Doing numbers 1 to 5 correctly will give you a mark of 13. Your teacher may give you only 11 or 12 marks if you have done them all but not particularly well.

6 Describe how you have used computers to measure or monitor external events.

   Doing numbers 1 to 6 correctly will give you a mark of 16. Your teacher may give you only 14 or 15 marks if you have done them all but not particularly well.

7 Explain why you have used a computer for this purpose.

   Doing numbers 1 to 7 correctly will give you a mark of 19. Your teacher may give you only 17 or 18 only marks if you have done them all but not particularly well.

Here is a series of tasks for you to do so that you can achieve mark boxes 1 to 7. Each task corresponds to a mark range. Task 1 gives you mark range 1; task 1 and task 2 give you mark range 2; tasks 1, 2 and 3 give you mark range 3 and so on.

TASK 1: Write about two devices you know about, which measure physical variables like temperature, sound, pressure, etc. This means that the devices must use sensors and timing devices. The sensors could be pressure sensors, temperature sensors, light sensors, sound sensors, moisture sensors, etc. You could write about how weather stations use sensors to monitor weather conditions or about measuring pollution in rivers or swimming baths. You could write about measuring the pH of soils.

Write down two examples of devices which use measurement. You must say what is being measured. You must also write about the sensor(s) being used. For example.

Device	What is being measured	Sensor being used
Weather station	The temperature outside	temperature sensor

You could write down that the temperature is being measured non-stop. The temperature sensor sends the measurement through an analogue-to-digital converter to a computer or microprocessor. The temperature is then stored in a database or spreadsheet.

TASK 2: All you need to do for this is to add two more examples to your list for task 1 and for each one add a description of how they work.

TASK 3: You will need to use a data logger connected to a computer or sensors connected to an interface which is connected to a computer.

- The sensors must be used to measure physical variables in an experiment.
- Use the system to measure or monitor things like temperature/pressure.
- You must write about how you connected all the equipment together.
- You will write up an experiment that you have carried out.
- You will need to take a photograph of the experiment and include it in your write-up.
- You must put labels on the photograph showing each piece of equipment.

(Your teacher will have done some work with you on measuring. All you have to do is to write about what you did in that lesson.)

TASK 4: You will need to get some printouts of the results of your experiment and write about how you got the computer to display the results of the measurements.

Supposing you were doing a simple experiment to measure the insulation properties of cups made of different materials. You will want to produce the cooling curves for each material. You will write about what software you used. You will then write about which options you used within the software in order to produce the graphs and the table of values. Make sure you print out the table and the graphs.

The graph may look something like this but you will need to print out the table as well. You will also need to label your axes and give it a title.

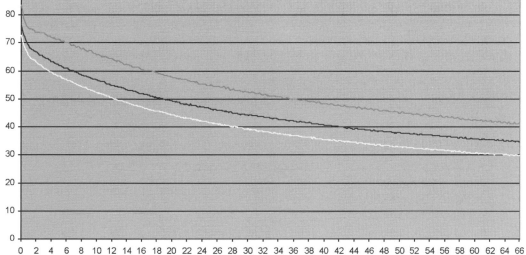

TASK 5: Having printed out your results you now need to explain what your results mean. Your graph is probably similar to the one above and now you must write about it. You must write down what the graph shows and also what your table of results mean.

You need to write about any trends you have noticed. In the graph above, the temperature of each cup drops quickly to begin with and then more slowly after a period of time. You need to say how quickly and how long it takes to slow down. Point this out on your graph. You need to say which of the three cups keeps its heat the longest. Use your table to write down the exact values. In your explanation you will write down:

● the initial temperature of each of the three cups;
● the drop in temperature over the first five seconds and the last five seconds;
● whether the temperature drops quickly or slowly over these times;
● the temperatures after 10 seconds, 20 seconds and so on;
● which cup is cooling the slowest, the fastest and in between.

TASK 6: You now have to write in a lot more detail how you used the equipment in the experiment. This write-up will need to include a description of:

● what the purpose of the experiment was – you will need to say why you are measuring what it is you are measuring;
● how the system measures analogue quantities – you will need to explain about the sensors you are using and which variables they are measuring;
● how the system converts the analogue data to digital data – you will need to explain how the interface you have connected the sensors to actually converts analogue data to digital;
● how it processes the data – you will need to write about what operations the software carries out such as timing, graphing and putting the results into a table;
● how it produces various types of output such as tables and graphs – you will write about the different forms of output which are possible e.g. text files, CSV files, Excel files, SID files, graphs.

✔ A D V I C E

In order to get a mark higher than 19 out of 28 for this strand you will need to create your own experiment. It will need to make use of two different types of sensor.

> Suggestions for measuring tasks

- Use suitable data logging equipment with a variety of sensors to conduct an investigation to determine the effect that age, gender and weight have on heart rate and blood pressure after mild exercise.

- Plot temperature, light and humidity over a 24-hour period.

- Observe transpiration in plants. Measure the temperature and changes in humidity of a plant.

Your work will need to include:

- a detailed description of how the investigation was carried out;
- a printout of the results;
- a conclusion supported by graphs and charts;
- an evaluation of the investigation.

How to get started

The guidance given here is about the transpiration task. You must use this as guidance to give you ideas and not just copy it out. That could lose you a lot of marks.

Setting out your work

You need to make your work easy for your teacher to mark and easy for the moderator to read. You will need to write up everything you have done. A good idea is to set out your work in different sections. The headings of each section are as follows:

- **Introduction**: In this section you will need to write a paragraph explaining what measuring means and why computers are needed. You will include examples of everyday devices which are used to measure variables. You will finish your introduction with a description of the experiment you are going to carry out.

- **Design of the experiment**: In this section you will draw the equipment you are going to use and write about the computer hardware and software you are going to use.

- **Construction of the experiment**: Here you will describe and include photographs of how you set up the experiment.

- **The results of the experiment**: Here you will print out and write about the results from the computer.

- **Conclusion**: In this section you will describe the important features and trends in your results and say what this means.

> What you need to do to get the marks

1 Load a word processor on your computer and type in a paragraph about computer measurement. Describe sensors and the need for analogue-to-digital conversion. Give four examples of everyday devices which are used in measuring. Write about what they are monitoring and what sensors they are using. You will need to mention the advantages of using computers rather than manual methods. Next you will type up the details of the experiment you are going to carry out. In your write-up make a list of the inputs to the system and the outputs from the system and what you expect to see. Type this under the heading **Introduction**.

You could explain how you are going to measure the humidity and temperature surrounding a plant in order to determine its rate of transpiration. You will need to give a general idea of what you expect to happen to the humidity and temperature over a period of time and what this will tell you about the transpiration of the plant.

2 In your **Design of the experiment** section you should design the experiment you are going to carry out. The next thing you will need to do is to draw a sketch showing the plant and how the sensors are going to be attached to it. You will need to draw a block diagram showing how the computer and interface will be connected with the sensors. You will also need to sketch the types of graph and tables you wish to create. These will just be rough ideas as at this stage you won't be certain about what these outputs are likely to look like. All this is to go under the heading **Design of the experiment**.

3 These are the next steps:

1 Take a photograph of the sensors. You can label this photograph which will help you later on when you write about the sensors.

2 Put a polythene bag over one of the branches of the plant.

3 Put the sensors inside the bag with the leads hanging outside the bag. Take a photograph of this set-up.

4 Plug the leads into the interface and take a photograph.

5 Connect the interface to the computer and take a photograph of the experiment.

Label the photographs you have taken and write in detail about how you constructed the experiment. Make sure you write at least a couple of sentences about each of the stages outlined above. All of this will go under the heading **Creation of the experiment**.

After all this you must decide which software you are going to use. Load it on to your computer and set up the time intervals. You must also select the form of output and this must include a table as well as a graph of results. Under the heading **Creation of the experiment** write a sentence about the software you have used. You should also write two or three lines about the hardware you have used.

4 Now you have to print out your results. You will probably have saved the data in spreadsheet form and will also have produced graphs. Get printouts of both the table and the graph. Put them under your heading **The results of the experiment**. You will also need to get a screenshot of your work area/folder showing how you saved the data. You must also describe how you used the measuring software to produce this file format.

Printed out your results and explain what your results mean. You need to write on your graph. Write down what the graph shows and what your table of results mean.

You need to write about any trends you have noticed. Look back at Step 5 above for some ideas about what we mean by trends. Point them out on your graph. You need to say how or if humidity or temperature increases or decreases over a period of time. In your written explanation you will write down:

- the initial temperature of the air surrounding the plant;
- the drop/increase in temperature over an initial short period of time;
- the drop/increase in humidity over an initial short period of time;
- whether the temperature drops or rises quickly or slowly over these times;
- whether the humidity drops or rises quickly or slowly over these times.

All this will go under the same heading, **The results of the experiment**.

5 You must now draw conclusions from the experiment. You need to say why the temperature drops or rises or stays the same. You must also say why you think the change (if there is one) is a rapid or slow change. You must do the same for humidity.

These conclusions must go under your **Conclusion** heading.

✔ A D V I C E

Doing *all* of numbers 1–5 correctly will give you a mark of 22. Your teacher may give you only 21 or 20 marks if you have done them all but not particularly well.

6 Next describe the sensors in more detail. You should already have labelled your photograph of the sensors. You just need to write a line or two about each one saying what you are using it to measure. This must go in your **Creation of the experiment** section.

7 You must store your results using more than one file format. You will need to describe how you have saved the displayed results. This will be a step-by-step guide to saving after the results are displayed. You will probably have used the format which comes with the software you used. The other section will describe how you exported the data to a spreadsheet or database package and then saved it in that format. You will need a screenshot of your work folder showing the file extensions. These may be of the form .txt, .sid, .csv, .plw, .emf, etc. This will go in your **The results of the experiment** section.

8 The final task is to give your reasons for choosing the hardware and software. You must give some good reasons. It could be that one type of software you considered did not allow you to save your results unless you copied and pasted them from an output window. The hardware chosen could be a remote data logger or one connected to a desktop or a laptop computer. You will need to say which and give two or three good reasons for your choice. The same number of reasons should be given for software. This should go at the appropriate place in your **Creation of the experiment** section.

An example project

Here is a project which achieved a mark of 25. Not all of the project is included. The fact that credit has been given below should not persuade you to miss anything out. Here is a list of items which are missing but would need to be present for 25 marks to be given.

There should be screenshots of the software menus and choices made in the **Construction of the Experiment** section. There should also be a lot more detail than shown here but these parts have been left out of this book due to copyright restrictions.

In the results section there should be screenshots of the data being recorded on screen as well as views of the graphs. There should also be screenshots of the save options. There should be a printout of the whole spreadsheet.

Here is a list of the criteria for 23 to 25 marks and where they were met in the project.

Criteria	Page
Describe how they have used computers to measure or monitor external events;	Page 1 onwards
Write about how everyday devices contain equipment which measure or monitor events;	Page 1
Give examples of some everyday devices which contain equipment which measure or monitor events;	Page 1
Design an experiment which uses measuring equipment to provide the solution to a given task;	Page 2
Construct the experiment and measure at least two different physical variables;	Pages 3, 4
Provide printouts and write about how the computer displayed the results of the measurements;	Pages 4, 5
Describe the types of sensors used;	Page 4
Explain the meaning of the displayed results;	Pages 6, 7
Store the displayed results using more than one file format.	Pages 4, 5

The project could not achieve a higher mark as there are no reasons given for the choice of hardware and software.

Acid-Base Titration

■ Introduction

My project is about measuring. I will use a computer to help me measure the pH and temperature of the results of adding an acid to a base. Temperature and pH can be measured without using a computer. You can put a thermometer in a liquid and read the temperature from it. There are also pH meters which can be used to measure pH.

The problem with these is that it needs a human to read the measurements. These readings are on scales which are not very easy to read. It is difficult to get an exact reading from a thermometer. This is because temperature is analogue. This means you are not really reading the temperature you are reading the distance that the mercury has risen inside a glass tube. When you use computers you have to use things called sensors which connect to the computer. Computers are better because they take digital readings and these are more precise. Because they work in digital data and variables like temperature are analogue the analogue data has to be changed to digital so the computer can understand it. This means that you can't just plug the sensors straight into the computer. An analogue-to-digital converter is used. This is often called the interface because it is between the sensors and the computer. You plug the sensors into the interface and the interface into the computer.

Computers are used to measure physical variables in weather stations. They are used to measure temperature, pressure, rainfall and wind speed/direction. They are better to use because they can take several readings at the same time, they don't need holidays and they can work all hours of the day and night. Instead of using things like thermometers, anemometers and barometers, temperature sensors, wind sensors and pressure sensors are used.

Another example of computer measurement is the use of blood pressure monitors by doctors. The old way used to be to take the readings from a mercury column but now a pressure sensor is used instead.

The police use breathalysers to catch drivers who drink and drive. They used to use machines where the driver would breathe into a plastic bag with chemicals. If the chemicals changed colour then they had been drinking too much. These days they use a breathalyser which has an alcohol sensor in it. This measures the amount of alcohol in the breath.

Noise pollution is monitored at airports. Using sound sensors, data is collected about the amount of noise. This is a very good example of humans not having to be in a very noisy area because computers are used.

■ My Experiment

I am going to set up an experiment to see what happens when an acid is added to a base. I know that the general result of this experiment is:

acid + base   ——————→   salt + water + heat

I am going to investigate the increase in temperature as well as looking at the pH levels. The pH of most strong acids is 2 or even lower. The pH for strong bases is 12 or more. My experiment will take readings of the pH and temperature of the liquid. The results will come on the screen as a table which I will print out. There will also be a graph which I will print out.

■ Design of the experiment

Here is my design of the experiment

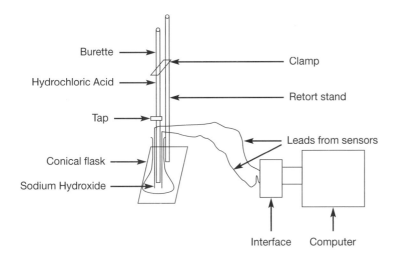

I will use a flask with a little sodium hydroxide in it. This will be placed flat on the base of the retort stand. I will use a clamp on the retort stand to hold the burette steady. It will go into the flask. The burette will contain the hydrochloric acid. I will get the technician to put the acid in the burette and the base in the flask as it is too dangerous for me to be handling these chemicals. I will also ask the technician to turn the tap in the burette on so that drops form and it goes gradually into the flask a drop at a time. The sensors will go in the flask and I must make sure that the leads don't go in as well. I will plug the leads into the buffer box (interface) and plug the buffer box into the computer.

I will run the software and it will have a table come on the screen. I will be able to choose it so that a graph comes up as well. I will be able to print these out.

My outputs will look like this:

Table of results

Time	pH graph	Temperature

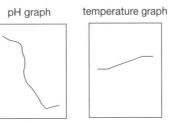

pH graph   temperature graph

■ Construction of the experiment

The first thing I did was to clamp the burette to the stand leaving enough room underneath for the flask to go. I got the technician to put the hydrochloric acid in the burette. He also put the sodium hydroxide in the flask and put it underneath the burette for me. Here is a photograph of the flask with the sodium hydroxide in it and the burette with acid in it.

Here is another photograph. This one shows the goggles I will need to wear. I don't want any alkali in my eyes!

The next thing I did was to connect the buffer box to the computer. I was using a laptop for this experiment.

Connecting lead from interface to laptop.

Buffer box

Laptop

I clamped the pH sensor to the stand and put it in the flask. I then plugged the other end into the buffer box.

The last thing to do was to put the temperature sensor in the flask and plug it into the buffer box.

Temperature sensor   pH sensor

③

I chose these two sensors because they will show the changes in the reaction. The temperature sensor will measure the temperature. As the heat increases with the reaction, it will warm up the solution. The temperature sensor will be used to get these increased readings to the computer by way of the buffer box. The pH sensor will measure the pH reading which will tell you whether the solution is still a base or if it is getting weaker or becoming acid.

The next step was to load up the software. I had to go to the menu and choose how often I wanted data recorded. I chose every second. I also chose the type of displays I wanted. I chose how long to record the data for. When I had finished it was time to look at my results.

The results of the experiment

In order to get a printout of the results the first thing I had to do was to save the data. I went to the File menu and clicked on 'Save As'. When the Save window opened I chose CSV for the file type but it saved as a text file.

I then loaded Excel and opened up the results file. I got this message so I clicked on next.

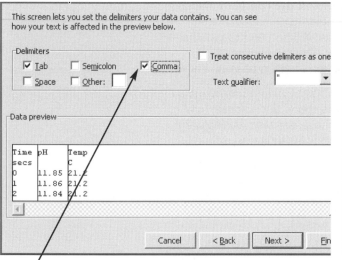

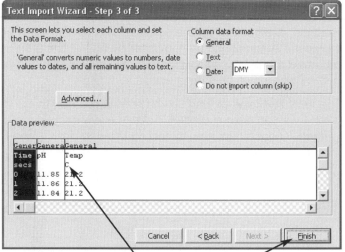

When this came up I clicked on Comma as it was a CSV (comma separated value) file.

When this came up I could see that everything was in its right column so I clicked on Finish.

	A	B	C	D
1	Time	pH	Temp	
2	secs		C	
3	0	11.85	21.2	
4	1	11.86	21.2	
5	2	11.84	21.2	
6	3	11.84	21.3	
7	4	11.85	21.3	
8	5	11.79	21.4	
9	6	11.71	21.4	
10	7	11.61	21.4	
11	8	11.51	21.4	
12	9	11.52	21.6	
13	10	11.43	21.7	
14	11	11.29	21.6	
15	12	11.14	21.7	
16	13	11.05	21.7	
17	14	11.07	21.7	
18	15	11.06	21.8	
19	16	11.01	21.8	
20	17	10.98	21.8	
21	18	10.97	21.8	
22	19	10.99	22	
23	20	10.83	22	
24	21	10.82	22.2	
25	22	10.71	22.3	

This shows you my table. Then I saved it as an Excel file.

When I had saved it, I then went to the graph icon and created graphs of pH against time and temperature against time.

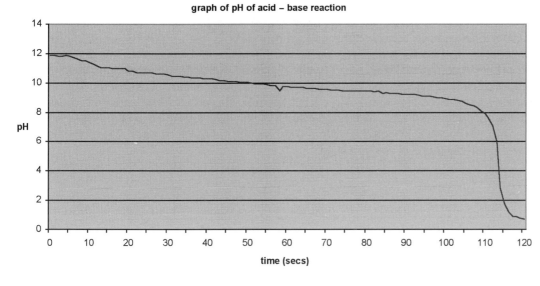

graph of pH of acid – base reaction

The initial pH of the solution was around the 11.85, 11.86 value but after only a few seconds of adding drops of acid the pH started to fall. Over the next 100 or so seconds it was falling slowly. It fell by an average of 0.03 per second. It didn't fall 0.03 every second this was just the average. Some seconds it fell by 0.1, others it didn't fall at all, in fact there were slight increases sometimes. After about 110 seconds it fell like a stone. The solution was only neutral (pH 7) for a second then it fell again because now all the sodium hydroxide was being used up and there was only water and hydrochloric acid in the solution.

The temperature gradually rose over the whole experiment although it did start to even out after 90 seconds. It started at 21.2 and rose to 25.9 before slowly cooling to 25.5.

107	8.43
108	8.31
109	8.09
110	7.89
111	7.56
112	7.11
113	5.99
114	2.81
115	1.76
116	1.19
117	0.88
118	0.91
119	0.79
120	0.71

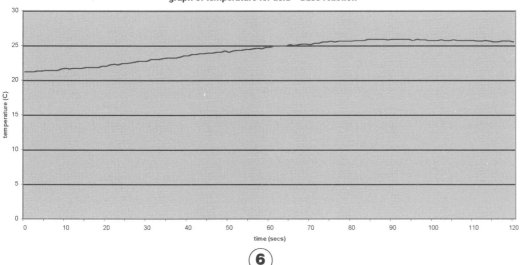

graph of temperature for acid – base reaction

■ Conclusion

The reaction of hydrochloric acid and sodium hydroxide does give salt and water and heat. This is proved by the pH going down (acids are low, bases are high and water is in the middle – pH7). When all the sodium hydroxide is used up there is nothing left to react so the hydrochloric acid just goes into the water and lies there. This is proved by the pH not stopping at 7 but going lower. When all the sodium hydroxide is used up the temperature stops going up. It starts to fall slightly after about 90 seconds. This isn't because there is no reaction going on but because there is so little sodium hydroxide left the reaction is smaller. The temperature is still hotter than room temperature because the reaction is going on. No more reaction takes place after 112 seconds so now the temperature is really falling.0

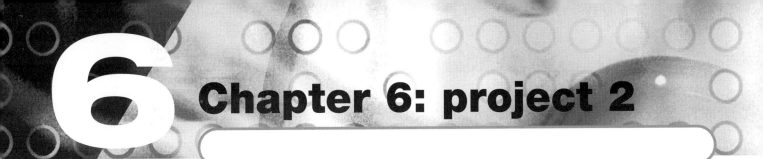

The marking of project 2 is different from projects 1a and 1b. It is divided into sections called:

- Analysis
- Design
- Implementation
- Testing
- User documentation
- Evaluation

Each of these sections is then divided into sub-sections. These sub-sections are usually marked out of 2, 3 or 4 marks.

In order to get the marks you do a certain amount of work to get 1 mark, if you add some more to it you get 2 marks. For sub-sections worth 3 marks you usually have to suggest alternative ideas. For sub-sections worth 4 marks you often have to give reasons for any choices you have made. This means that you have to know what is needed for 1 mark before you start. **You cannot miss out any steps in your work.**

> What you have to do for project 2

You have to identify a problem which you are going to solve by producing an Information System **for others to use**. For this reason it is not a good idea to use word processing or desktop publishing as a theme. If you did so you would have to concentrate on creating templates and designs of documents rather than just the documents themselves. Many students find this extremely difficult to visualise so you would be well advised to leave these alone. The system will usually be a database or a spreadsheet. To gain high marks, however, you will need to use at least two different pieces of software to solve your problem.

The best way to identify a problem is if you can think of an organisation or individual that needs a computer system to help them with the way they work. They may not have a computer at all at the moment. The organisation can be something as simple as a clothes shop, a sports shop, a phone shop, a youth club, a local football club. If you choose an individual it must be someone who needs an information system for their work such as the head of a school P.E. department who wants to keep a list of sports stock and pupil records on computer. It must not be somebody like your best friend who just wants to keep records of all their videos, DVDs or CDs! If you can't think of a problem yourself your teacher will give you a list of possible problems and you can choose one. Remember to put the list in with your work when you have finished.

On the next two pages you will see a list of tasks which are recommended by OCR. For the purpose of explaining how to do project 2, task 3 – the video rental shop – will be used as an example. You must use this as guidance to give you ideas and not just copy it out. That could lose you a lot of marks.

> Suggestions for project 2 tasks

1 Devise a system that would help the owner of a car dealership to organise the business. There are several aspects to the business that the owner needs help with.
  - A record of all the stock has to be kept so that if a customer comes in and make enquiries about a specific car, salesmen can immediately inform them whether the dealership has such a car.

- A record of customers has to be kept for further mailings about special offers.
- The servicing department has to keep a record of all the parts in the stores.
- Itemised bills have to be prepared for customers when they have their cars serviced (certain customers are allowed a discount).

Choose one or more of these aspects of the business when devising your solution. In order to gain high marks, at least two aspects of the business will need to be considered.

2 Devise a system that would help the managers of a leisure centre/fitness club to provide a more efficient service to their members. There are several aspects of the leisure centre/fitness club that they need help with.
- Keep a record of every member's details.
- Measure the heart rate, blood pressure and other physiological measures of the members after various set exercises.
- Compare these measures with national norms and advise their members on their fitness levels.
- Keep a record of their members' fitness levels to produce charts showing their progress.
- Send details of centre/club activities.

Choose one or more of these aspects of the activities of the organisers when devising your solution. To gain high marks, at least two aspects of the centre need to be considered.

3 Devise a system that would help the owner of a video rental shop to organise his business. There are several aspects to the business that he needs help with.
- A record of all the videos has to be kept so that if a customer comes in and makes enquiries about a specific video, shop assistants can immediately inform them whether they have it in the shop at that time.
- A record of customers has to be kept with the videos they have on hire so that overdue notices can be sent if required.
- The various pricing strategies have to be calculated so that special offers, such as 'hire three get one free', can be applied.
- Letters can be sent to customers if a new film, which matches their particular preferences, comes into the shop.

Choose one or more of these aspects of the business when devising your solution. In order to gain high marks, at least two aspects of the business will need to be considered.

Your solution to any of the above tasks should include the following:

- identification of problems with the current system;
- interviews with potential users of such a system;
- documents/forms and methods of measuring in use in the current system;
- identification of the inputs, outputs and processing currently employed;
- designs of the structure of databases/spreadsheets/word processing documents/ data-logging equipment required;
- design of the input screens and the output documents/screens of the new computerised system;
- documentation of the databases/spreadsheets/word processing documents/data logging systems and how the associated input screens and output documents/screens were created;
- the combination of the outputs from one piece of software into another;
- evidence of testing;
- a User Guide showing how to use the new system;
- an evaluation of the final system compared with the original design.

Setting out your work

You need to make your work easy for your teacher to mark and easy for the moderator to read. You will need to write up everything you have done. A good idea is to set out your work in different sections. You will need to use the headings which were shown above:

- **Introduction:** In this section you will need to describe the organisation or individual and what they do. You should explain why the system is needed.

- **Analysis:** Here you will describe the problems with the system as it is now and describe how you intend to collect information about the current system. You will end the section by describing the type of system which you are recommending to solve the problems.

- **Design:** Here you will describe the structure of the database or spreadsheet or the word processing templates you are going to create and describe how the user will enter data into the system. You will describe the form that the output will take and what it will consist of.

- **Implementation:** Here you will describe how you created your database or spreadsheet or word processing templates. Go into a lot of detail about the software features you used to create them and use screenshots to demonstrate how you created them.

- **Testing:** Here you will describe how you tested the system you created and describe your test plan. You will need to use a variety of data and describe what happened as a result of the tests. You will need to include printouts of the results of your tests.

- **User documentation:** In this section you will describe how someone could use your system. You will tell them, step-by-step, how to enter, change and save data as well as showing them how to use your system to do searches or whatifs or create standard letters, etc.

- **Evaluation:** In this section you will describe how your system compares with the original problem, your design. You will describe any limitations or suggested improvements as well as evaluating your system from the point of view of a potential user of your system.

> What you need to do to get the marks

Let us look at task 3 about a video rental shop. You must write about what the shop does and how the current system works.

Write down under the heading **Introduction**:

- the name of the shop and where it is located;
- how many people work there;
- how many videos or DVDs are in the shop and how many customers there are;
- how many videos or DVDs are out on rental on a typical day.
- the prices to rent videos or DVDs and also how many days they can be borrowed for;
- i.e. special offers, renting a video or DVD for three days and only having to pay two days rental.

Analysis

In your **Analysis** section you must write about the problems with the current system and how the shop assistants cope with these. You will write about the system they use at the moment. In order to do this you will need to collect information about the system as it is used at the moment. For this reason you may find it easier if you do the 1a tasks and 1b tasks together.

You will also need to write about what the shop assistants will need from a computer system. This will be a list of the things that a computer could do for them but which they are finding it difficult to do at the moment. This will help you later to design a new system.

Here is a list of tasks which you will need to carry out to get marks for the analysis of your problem. Use the subheadings given below and put all your work for each subheading in your **Analysis** section.

For tasks A1(i) to A1(iv) you will use the subheadings **The Problem** and **The User's Requirements**.

For A2(i) to A2(iv) you will use the subheading **Collecting Information**.

For A3(i) to A3(iv) you will use the subheadings **Inputs, Outputs, Processing** and **System Specification**.

TASK A1(I):   Write down a list of problems. This might start:

- when a customer comes in and asks about a certain video or DVD, shop assistants have difficulty finding out whether it is out on rental or not;
- at some point in the day one of the shop assistants has to look through the borrowers' records to see if any borrower has a video or DVD which is overdue.

A satisfactory list for this task would have two or three more problems. Put this under the subheading **The Problem**. Doing A1(i) successfully will get you 1 mark.

TASK A1(II):   Now you need to make a list of user requirements. The list could start like this:

The user needs a system which will help her to easily:
- find out which comedy films are still in the shop and not out on rental;
- produce a list of all the users who have videos or DVDs which are overdue.

Your list will need to be a lot longer than this. Put it under the subheading **The User's Requirements**. Doing A1(i) and A1(ii) successfully will get you 2 marks.

TASK A1(III):   Now you need to write about how the shop assistants deal with each problem listed in A1. This is a possible start:

At the moment all the information about each video or DVD is written on sheets of paper. Each sheet of paper has the details of about 20 videos/DVDs with the code number for each video or DVD. When a customer comes in and ask about a certain video or DVD, shop assistants have to look through these sheets of paper to see if it is out on rental or not. If the customer doesn't know the number of the video or DVD (which is common) then the shop assistant has to look through every sheet until she gets to the right one.

The details of all the customers are also kept on separate sheets of paper with about 10 customers to a page. The details of each customer will include the code numbers of any videos or DVDs they have borrowed, the date borrowed and the date due back. At some point the shop assistant has to make a list of all the customers who have overdue videos or DVDs. She has to look through all the pieces of paper with the borrowers' records on to see if the due back date has been passed.

- You will need to describe how the shop assistant deals with the four or five problems which you listed for Task A1 (i). Put this under the subheading **The Problem**.

You must also add more detail to what you wrote for A1(ii). It might start:

The user needs a system which will help her to easily:
- find out which comedy films are still in the shop and not out on rental. This will be a list giving the code numbers, video/DVD titles, main stars and so on;
- produce a list of all the users who have videos or DVDs which are overdue. This will show their names, addresses and phone numbers.

You will need to add more detail to every item on your list in A1(ii). Put it under the subheading **The User's Requirements**. Doing A1(i), A1(ii) and A1(iii) successfully will get you 3 marks.

TASK A1(IV): The list of problems in A1(i) seem to suggest that a computer database will be needed for the solution. Your list for A1(i) will now need to have two or three more problems added. These extra problems would need another piece of software to solve them. Your solution may need a database and a word processor or spreadsheet.

It could be that at the moment it is difficult to send out letters to customers who have videos or DVDs overdue. You will need to say why this is so. There might also be a problem sending letters to customers who might be interested in certain types of film when a new film of that type comes into the shop. Again, you will need to say why this is so.

You will now need to describe how the shop assistant deals with these two or three extra problems. This will be a follow-on from what you did for A1(iii) but will refer to the extra problems you have added to your list. Put this under the subheading **The Problem**.

You need to add to your list for A1(iii). You will write down the user requirements for your extra two or three problems. Put it under the subheading **The User's Requirements**.

Doing A1, A1(ii), A1(iii) and A1(iv) successfully will get you 4 marks.

●● COLLECTING INFORMATION

TASK A2(I): You must collect information from people who use the system at the moment. This will be the manager and the shop assistants. The information which you collect must be about the current system and how it works. You will need to show how you collected this information or documents currently being used. The information you collect must help you to describe the problems that the current users face. You will ask them to describe exactly how they find details of borrowers and video or DVD titles and what information is kept about borrowers and films, etc. You will not ask them to tell you what fields they would like on a database, for example. This section is all about you analysing the problem(s). You will find a solution to their problems and at this stage you have not decided whether or not they even need a database.

You must provide evidence that you have used at least one method of collecting information from the users of the current system. Many students lose marks here because they go to all the trouble of producing questionnaires and describe in great detail how they gave them out. However, they then fail to include in their work the questionnaires which have been filled in.

- If you have interviewed the manager and shop assistants you will need to produce transcripts of the interviews and put them in your **Collecting information** section.
- If you have given them questionnaires to fill in, you will need to include the completed questionnaires in this section.

- If you have written to the manager you must include the replies from the manager in this section. Just saying that he or she never wrote back is not enough. If you don't get any replies you will have to use another method of collecting information.
- If you have gathered together documents which are currently used by the shop you must put these in this section.
- If you have been to the shop to observe the shop assistants and manager at work, you will include a list of things which you saw such as how they looked for records, etc. You must put the list in this section.

Doing A2(i) successfully will get you 1 mark.

TASK A2(II):   You are now required to describe how you obtained the information. This will go into your **Collecting Information section**. This is, obviously, in addition to what you have already included in this section for task A2(i).

If you have interviewed the manager and shop assistants you will need to write about how it took place. You will need to write about:
- how you arranged the interviews;
- where they took place;
- the time and date they took place;
- how you might have changed some questions depending on what you found out.

If you have given them questionnaires to fill in, you will need to write about:
- how you created the questionnaire;
- what questions you decided not to include;
- why you chose the questions which you did include;
- when you gave them out and when you received the completed questionnaires;
- how you analysed the results.

If you have sent letters to video shops. You will write about:
- how you created the letter;
- what you decided to ask about in your letter;
- why you asked those questions;
- who you sent the letters to.

If you've gathered documents currently used by the shop you will write about:
- where you got them from;
- when you got them and who gave them to you;
- which particular documents you were looking for and why you wanted them.

If you have observed the shop assistants and manager you will write about:
- the list of things that you would be looking to see the manager and assistants do;
- when you went to the shop;
- what you actually saw;
- what you made notes about as you were watching.

You will also need to write about how the collected information helped you to work out the current problems facing the manager and shop assistants.

Doing A2(i) and A2(ii) successfully will get you 2 marks.

TASK A2(III): As well as what you have put in your **Collecting information** section so far you will also need to write about alternative methods of collecting information. Whichever method you have chosen you will write about at least two other ways you could have collected information.

If you used questionnaires you need to write about how you could have got the same information by writing letters, by interviewing the users, by obtaining copies of documents or by observing the users. You need to describe these in a little detail.

Doing A2(i), A2(ii) and A2(iii) successfully will get you 3 marks.

TASK A2(IV): The last section is where you write down some advantages and some disadvantages of using your chosen method. You also write down advantages and disadvantages of the alternative methods. This will help you to explain why you chose the method you used.

One of the reasons you might give is to describe how you thought about interviewing the shop assistants but you felt that it would take too long to arrange and complete all the interviews. There would be an advantage in using questionnaires to get the same information as you could give them out one week and collect them all the following week.

This, of course, is only one advantage with one alternative method. You need to write about advantages and disadvantages and do this with two alternative methods as well as your own. The advantages must be greater than the disadvantages otherwise your teacher, not to say the moderator, may well ask why you chose your method!

Doing A2(i), A2(ii), A2(iii) and A2(iv) successfully will get you 4 marks.

TASK A3(I): The next two tasks are about identifying the inputs, outputs and processing required by the system. This means that you should still be writing about the current system, not the new system which you should not have decided upon yet.

Under the heading **Inputs, Outputs, Processing** write down:

A list of the inputs to the current system.

> Inputs which would need to go on the list would be based on questions a customer might ask in the shop. The inputs would be queries along the lines of 'Have you got?':
> - a comedy film for £2.00 or less.
> - a horror film starring Christopher Lee.
> - a film directed by Steven Spielberg for £1.50 (or less).

> Other inputs which would need to go on the list would be based on the shop assistants or managers requirements:
> - so that customers with a certain name could be found.
> - customers with a certain type of preference could be found.
> - overdue videos.

A list of the outputs from the current system. These would be the outputs resulting from the inputs mentioned above.

> Outputs which would need to go on the list could be:
> - The titles, types and prices of comedy films for £2.00 or less.
> - The titles and directors of horror films starring Christopher Lee.
> - The titles, actors and prices of films directed by Steven Spielberg for £1.50 or less.

Other outputs which would need to go on the list could be:

- names of customers being looked for.
- Names and types of videos and customer names and addresses.
- Names of videos, date borrowed, number of days overdue, name and address of customers

A list of the processing requirements of the current system.

One item on the list could be:

- For the first example above the shop assistant will search through the comedy films looking for those that are £2.00 or less.
- You will need to do this for all the above examples.

Doing A3(i) successfully will get you 1 mark.

TASK A3(II): You now need to go into more detail about what you have written so far. You will find it easier if you describe the inputs, outputs and processing together.

For example you might write about how a customer might come into the shop and want to hire a comedy film but does not want to pay more than £2. The manager will have to search through the files for all the comedy films. He/she will then search through all these comedy films for those which are £2 or less to hire. Having found all the videos which match these conditions, he/she writes down the prices, titles and types of these videos or DVDs. In conclusion you must now write down that the input data was the price and type of the video. The processing was the searching for the matching type and price. The output is the title and price of the matching films.

You must write about the other examples you mentioned in task A3(i) and what the inputs, processing and outputs will be for these.

Your work for task A3(ii) will follow on from your work for task A3(i) under the heading **Inputs, Outputs, Processing.**

Doing A3(i) and A3(ii) successfully will get you 2 marks.

TASK A3(III): Your work for tasks A3(iii) and A3(iv) will go under a new heading **System Specification.**

Now that you have completed your analysis of the problems faced by the manager and shop assistants you must decide on what type of system you think you will need. This only needs to be a rough guide as, at this stage, you will not be certain of the exact solution to these problems. The exact specification of your proposed system will only become definite after you have designed your solution.

- The first thing to do is to write down the software you are going to use. From what we have seen so far you will need a database. This will store the records of the videos. At this point you don't have to say exactly which software you are going to use. You will also need a word processor to produce the letters to customers.

- Now you need to write down the hardware which you think will be needed.

Doing A3(i), A3(ii) and A3(iii) successfully will get you 3 marks.

TASK A3(IV): Now that you have written about the hardware and software which will be needed, you must now write about an alternative specification. Make sure you write about alternative hardware and software. Many students lose this mark because they only give alternative hardware or alternative software. You must give both.

You need to write down the reasons why the specification you have chosen would be better than the alternatives. The reasons must be related to the problem you are solving and not just because they are more modern and have bigger memory, faster speed etc.

You might want to choose a cheaper, more simple to use system than a more up to date one because the manager and shop assistants might not be used to using computers. They might need an easier to use system rather than the latest system.

Doing A3(i), A3(ii), A3(iii) and A3(iv) successfully will get you 4 marks.

Design

In your **Design** section you must now write about your proposed solution to the problems with the current system. You will design input screens, output formats and file structures as well as deciding on the computer hardware and software you are recommending to the manager and shop assistants.

Here is a list of tasks which you will need to carry out to get marks for the Design of your solution. They are labelled D1(i) to D4(iii). Use the subheadings given below and put all your work for each subheading in your **Design** section.

For tasks D1(i) to D1(iii) you will use the subheading **Data structure**.
For D2(i) to D2(iii) you will just use the subheading **User interface**.
For D3(i) to D3(iii) you will use the subheading **Output formats**
For D4(i) to D4(iii) you will use the subheading **Software and hardware requirements**

TASK D1(I): This task must be written out under the heading **Data Structure**. You now need to produce a file structure for your database. The best way to do this is to use a word processor to create a table. Do not use database software to do this. There are two reasons for this. One is that at the moment you are in the design stage of the solution and using the database software comes at the implementation stage. The second, and most important, reason is that you have not decided on the database software you are going to use yet. This comes at the end of the design stage. You cannot make the decision until you have decided on the designs of the inputs, outputs and processing. Only then can you say which software would be the best one to implement these designs.

A design for the video database would be the field names, field types, field lengths and validation checks you are going to use on your database.

Field name	Field type	Field length	Validation
Title	Text	40	
Genre	Text		
Price		<10	

You will need to use the fields you wrote about in your **Analysis** section. Only some examples have been given here. The field types and lengths must be appropriate and not just written down without any thought.

You will need to produce a similar design for the customer database and also the structure of the standard letter template.

Doing D1(i) successfully will get you 1 mark.

TASK D1(II): You need to produce alternative designs to the structures produced. It is sufficient to produce an alternative design for each of two structures. In other words, you only have to produce one alternative design to your Videos database and one alternative to your Customers database.

A good idea would be to get hold of some videos or DVDs and find out what information is given on the sleeve. You could look at some blank membership forms at your local video shop to see what information is kept about the members.

You may feel that the membership number for the customer might be included in the Videos database. You might want to change one or two of the field types. You might think that a drop-down list for the owners to choose from would be better than them typing in the data (for some of the fields). You may feel that, having looked at a selection of videos/DVDs extra fields may be needed. You must write about all this. Because you have to describe your designs, it is a good idea to write down why you have chosen each field in your original and alternative databases (Videos and Customers). All this must be done immediately after task D1(i) under the heading **Data structure**.

Doing D1(i) and D1(ii) successfully will get you 2 marks.

TASK D1(III): You must now write down the advantages and disadvantages of each structure. This means you would be well advised to write down a couple of advantages and disadvantages of each structure. You will write a one or two line conclusion saying which designs you have chosen and why. You will write all this immediately after your work for task D1(ii) under the heading **Data structure**.

Doing D1(i), D1(ii) and D1(iii) successfully will get you 3 marks.

TASK D2(I): The next part of your write-up will be under a new heading **User interface**. You must produce a design for your user interface. This will contain the same fields as your final data structure design. You must concentrate on the layout. The things you need to be concerned with are:

- the size of the fields;
- the size of the field names;
- the position of the fields and field names;
- a title;
- the font and font size.

Here is a design for part of the input screen (user interface) for the Video file, as an example. Because it is an input screen you will need to include all the fields.

The first idea here is to use the same font and font size throughout such as Arial size 11. As you can see, it is very easy to read. The size of the boxes for each field have been made big enough so that there will be enough room if all the field length is used (e.g. Description has a box big enough for 100 characters to fit in).

Doing D2(i) successfully will get you 1 mark.

TASK D2(II): Still under the heading **User interface** you must now create an alternative design. You must not try and change the fields or field lengths at this stage as this screen design must contain the same fields as your final data structure design. You are only going to change the layout and the size of the fonts and boxes. There must be good reasons for doing this. You cannot change them just for the sake of it. You may think that one or two fields should be moved closer to the top of the screen. In the example below, the customer number has been moved to the top as the manager might feel that this is a vital piece of information. He may think that this needs to go next to the title. He may also think that making the price box bigger would make it clear to the shop assistants that when they are entering data in this field they cannot afford to make mistakes.

Second design for user interface:

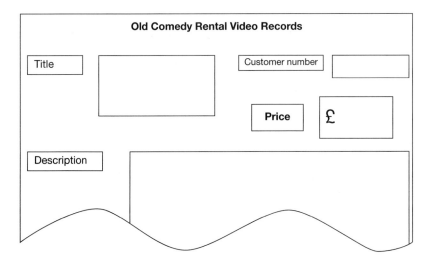

Doing D2(i) and D2(ii) successfully will get you 2 marks.

TASK D2(III): Now you must write down the advantages and disadvantages of each design. You will then give reasons for your choice. For the designs above one advantage of design 1 is that all the fields are neatly spaced out. One disadvantage is that there is no heading for the screen telling you whether it is the customer or video file.

For design 2 one advantage is that the number box is large enough to make it look important. A disadvantage is that because the customer number box has moved to the top the box showing the actors will be lower down.

You would be well advised to write down a couple of advantages and disadvantages of each screen. You must then explain which is going to be your final design. You will write all this immediately after your work for task D2(ii).

Doing D2(i), D2(ii) and D2(iii) successfully will get you 3 marks.

TASK D3(I): The next part of your write-up will be under a new heading **Output formats**. You will produce a design for one of your outputs. This can contain a selection of fields from your database. It would be best if you concentrated on deciding what type of report you would need if you were printing out the results of a query. This time you can decide on which fields you are going to use, but, as with your user interface, you will need to pay special attention to the layout. The things you need to be concerned with are:

- the fields to be printed out;
- the font and font size of the headings and data;
- whether it is going to be a table, individual records or some other type of output.

Here is a design for part of a report (output format) for the Customer file, based on a query which might be asked about the details of people with overdue videos.

Customer Number	Surname	First Names	Title of video
12345	Jones	William, Alfred	Harry Potter
23456	Davis	Wilfred	The Life

You need to write about which fields you have used and why, the type of layout you have used (in this case, a table), the fonts you have used and why as well as writing about the query that this report (output format) is based on. These reports must not be based on options available within a software package. You should be able to design these yourself so that when you implement them you do not have to rely on the use of wizards.

Doing D3(i) successfully will get you 1 mark.

TASK D3(II): The next thing to do, just like you did for your user interface, is to create an alternative design. This will follow on from the previous task under the heading **Output formats**. You may feel that it is quite likely that the manager will need to write a letter to the customer telling them that the video is overdue. A different set of fields may need to be printed out so that the address can be copied or printed on to an envelope. You may also need to change the layout and the size of the fonts to fit on an envelope.

Here is a possible second design:

First Names	William, Alfred
Surname	Jones
Address1	2, Hardington Drive
Address2	Curzon Valley
City	Dodminster

Doing D3(i) and D3(ii) successfully will get you 2 marks.

TASK D3(III): Immediately after completing tasks D3(i) and D3(ii), you must write down the advantages and disadvantages of each design. You will then give reasons for your choice. For the designs above, one advantage of design 1 is that, because of the layout, you can see all the people who have videos overdue. One disadvantage is that there may not be enough space for all the fields you need if you set it out this way.

For design 2 one advantage is that this layout would allow you to send out reminders as you can include all the contact details you need without running out of space on the paper. A disadvantage is that the field names are also printed out and you wouldn't need them if you were copying all the details onto an envelope.

Again you will find it easier to get this mark if you write down two advantages and two disadvantages of each report (output format). You can then explain which is going to be your final design.

Doing D3(i), D3(ii) and D3(iii) successfully will get you 3 marks.

TASK D4(I): The next task will be under a new heading **Software and hardware requirements**. Having decided on the solution to your problem you must now write down items of software and hardware. This list must be essential for the solution of the problem.

Your list may include the following:
- the type of processor you think will be needed.
- the minimum speed of processor which you think will be adequate.
- the amount of internal memory (RAM) which will be needed.
- the operating system you feel will be necessary, such as an up to date version of Windows. You must, however, say which version.
- the size of hard disk in gigabytes.
- the type of printer (laser, deskjet, etc.).
- any other input and output devices you may feel are needed.
- the database software which you have chosen.
- the word processing software you have chosen.

You can now mention brand names and be specific about types of computer system.

You must not forget to mention the software. If you only list the hardware you will not gain this mark or the marks for tasks D4(ii) and D4(iii).

Doing D4(i) successfully will get you 1 mark.

TASK D4(II): Immediately after your work for task D4(i), you must now write about an alternative computer system. These may be alternative types of computer and software available in school or at home. These must be sensible alternatives and not just listed for the sake of it. There may be alternative types of printer which incorporate scanners which you may have already mentioned the need for. There may be alternative input devices which could be used to input the customers' details. There must also be mention of an alternative software package.

Doing D4(i) and D4(ii) successfully will get you 2 marks.

TASK D4(III): You must now choose between these alternative information systems. You must justify the system you have chosen. You will list the good points about both systems as well as the bad points of both systems. You will write about how there are more good points about the chosen system than the alternative. You will also, hopefully, write about how there are fewer bad points regarding the chosen system than the alternative. One reason (but there will need to be many) you could give is to refer to a difference in hard disc space. You could say how it is essential to have a large hard disc space as you will be storing lots of images (scanned images such, as the front cover of each video). You need to give reasons for both your choice of hardware and software.

Doing D4(i), D4(ii) and D4(iii) successfully will get you 3 marks.

Implementation

Having finalised your designs you are now ready to move on to creating your solution. You would first of all create your file structures for the Customer file and the Videos file. You would then create the structure of your standard letters. You will write about how you did this under the heading **Implementing the data structure**. The four tasks **I1(i)** to **I1(iv)** described below will show you how to get up to four marks for this section. After this you will create your user interface and output formats. You will write about this under the heading **Implementing the input and output formats**. There are another four tasks described below numbered **I2(i)** to **I2(iv)** which will show you how to get up to four marks for this section. Your teacher will also award you marks for your use of the different software packages. There are no tasks written especially for this but you can think of the marks as **I3(i)** to **I3(iv)** and **I4(i)** to **I4(ii)** and the points at which these marks can be achieved will be indicated below. These marks can crop up in your two implementation sections and the testing section. The only extra writing you have to do in the implementation section is to gain the mark **I3(iv)**. You will need to write down the reasons for choosing to use the software features you used rather than other possible features. This is probably done more easily in the **Implementing the input and output formats** section than the others.

You can only gain marks for **I1** and **I2** if you have implemented the final designs which you documented in your **Design** section. It cannot be something different which you then change to match your design.

TASK I1(I): Under the heading **Implementing the data structure** you must write a brief description about how you created your solution. Don't copy down this list word for word as there are missing steps and there are gaps where the names of files/software should go. You will write about how you:

● loaded the software, e.g. *I moved the mouse pointer over the zzzzz icon and ...*
● used the software to create a new file called Videos, e.g. *I clicked on Blank datafile and ...*
● typed in the field names, data types, lengths and validation checks, e.g. *First of all in the first row under the Field name column I typed in video title then ...*
● saved the design, e.g. *When I had finished typing all my field names, types, lengths and validation checks I ...*

You need to do this for the Videos file, Customers file and standard letter.

Doing task I1(i) successfully will get you 1 mark. It will also get you the mark for I3(i).

TASK I1(II): Still using the heading **Implementing the data structure** you need to make quite a detailed description of how you created your solution. This means that somebody who knows something about computers should be able to produce the same database structure after reading your description. You can get a friend to follow what you've written and see if they can produce the same structure.

The best way of doing this is by adding screenshots to your descriptions. Again, don't be tempted to copy down word for word what follows as there are missing steps. To get I1(i) you could miss out some of the steps but in order to complete I1(ii) you can't miss out any steps.

● load the software e.g, *I moved the mouse pointer over the zzzzz icon and ...*

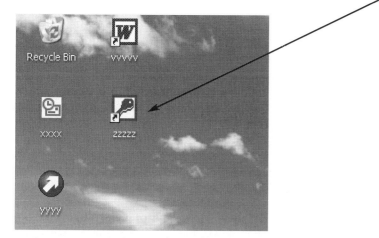

● used the software to create a new file called Videos. e.g, *I clicked on Blank datafile and ...*

Every step you write about should have a screenshot to go with it.

If you do task I1(ii) successfully you will get 2 marks.

TASK I1(III): Now you must write about any changes you made to the structure which make it different to the structure you produced in your **Design** section.

This part of the write-up comes under the heading **Implementing the data structure**.

The changes could be extra fields that have been added to your database such as **number of days borrowed for** in the Videos database. The address in the customer database might need to be split up into separate lines and a postcode. It could be that the field types have been changed such as the customer number might be treated as text rather than a number.

You will need to write about two or three such changes and they must be necessary and not just made up. You will need to include screenshots showing how you used the software to make the changes.

If you do I1(i) and I1(iii) successfully you will get 3 marks.

TASK I1(IV): Here you need to write about why it was necessary to make these changes. You might explain that you needed to include the number of days borrowed so the computer could calculate whether the video was overdue. You need to write down the search criteria for an overdue video. This would clearly show why this field is necessary and that you understand its use. You must write in detail about your other changes.

If you do I1(ii), I1(iii) and I1(iv) successfully you will get 4 marks.

TASK I2(I): Under the heading **Implementing the input and output formats** you will now write a brief description about how you created your input screens and printed reports. Don't forget you must not copy down this list word for word as there are missing steps. You will write about how you:

● used the software to create a new input form, e.g. *I clicked on forms and ...*
● selected the field names to go on the form, e.g. *First of all instead of choosing individual fields I ...*
● chose the layout and colours, e.g. *I clicked on OK and I ...*

You need to do this for the Videos file and the Customers file.

You must then do the same for the printed reports. You will start off by showing how you created a simple query and then created a report form. You will write about how you:

● used the software to create a new report, e.g. *I clicked on reports and ...*
● selected the field names to go on the report, e.g. *I decided that the fields I would need to print out would be ... so I ...*
● chose the layout and colours, e.g. *I clicked on OK and I ...*

Just like the forms, you need to do this for the Videos file and the Customers file.

Doing task I2(i) successfully will get you 1 mark.

TASK I2(II): Still using the heading **Implementing the input and output formats** you need to make quite a detailed description of how you created your forms and reports. Just as before, this means that somebody who knows something about computers should be able to produce the same forms and reports after reading your description. Use a friend to try it out.

It would be a good idea to add screenshots to your descriptions. Again, don't be tempted to copy down word for word what follows as there are missing steps. You could afford to miss out some of the steps for I2(i) but you cannot miss out any steps if you want to get the mark for I2(ii). You will write about how you:

- used the software to create a new input
  form, e.g. *I clicked on Forms and ...*

- used the software to create a new report,
  e.g. *I clicked on Reports and ...*

Every step you write about must have a screenshot to go with it.

If you do task I2(ii) successfully you will get 2 marks.

TASK I2(III): Now it is time to write about any changes you made to the input
and output formats which make them different to the formats you produced in your
Design section.

This part comes under the heading **Implementing the input and output formats.**

For the input screens the changes could be that the shape of some of the larger fields
have been changed. They could either be stretched out into a long rectangle or
squashed up into a square. The colours of certain fields could have been changed.
For the output formats the field names could have been removed and just the field
contents left.

You will need to write about two or three such changes and they must be necessary
and not just made up. You will need to include screenshots showing how you used
the software to make the changes.

If you do I2(ii) and I2(iii) successfully you will get 3 marks.

TASK I2(IV): For this task you need to write about why it was necessary to make
these changes. You might write about sending letters to customers with overdue
videos. You would not want the field names on the envelope just the field contents.
You must write as much detail about your other changes.

If you do I2(ii), I2(iii) and I2(iv) successfully you will get 4 marks.

MARKS FOR I3(I) TO I4(II):

- If you do task I1(i) or I1(ii) successfully you will get the mark for I3(i).
- Creating a database structure, an input form, a query and a report will get you the mark for I3(ii).
- Creating a database structure, an input form, a query, a report and a standard letter will get you the mark for I3(iii).
- For I3(iv) you must explain why you chose to use certain software features instead of using others. You could give reasons why you thought it was necessary to use input forms rather than typing the data into a table, or give reasons why you thought it was necessary to use reports rather than just printing out the results of a query.
- For I4(i) you will need to show how you transferred data from the database package to the word processor. You will need to show how you set up a mail merge to produce a letter to customers who had overdue videos. This will need screenshots of how you did it. You will also need to print out two copies of the letter, one before and one after the mail merge.
- For I4(ii) you could do another mail merge but it must be for a separate purpose, different to the overdue videos. You will need to show as much detail as for I4(i).

Testing

This section is about showing that your solution works. There are 7 marks available for this section we will call these marks **T1(i)**, **T1(ii)**, **T1(iii)**, **T1(iv)**, **T2(i)**, **T2(ii)** and **T2(iii)**.

The first thing you must do is to draw a table showing your test plan. It will have three columns. The test to be carried out, the expected results of the test and the actual test results. These must include things you have written about in the **User's requirements** section.

Test	Expected Results	Actual results
All comedy videos	What women want Throw Momma from the train Mars Attacks Private's Progress Smokey and the Bandit Vicar of Dibley	See printout 1

If you do this for every test you carried out you will get the mark for T2(i).

To get the mark for **T1(i)** you would need to print out the query conditions and write about what you are looking for.

Then you would print out the results of the query.

To get the mark for **T1(ii)** you must do at least two queries. You would need to print out the query conditions and write about what you are looking for. These would also be put in your test plan table.

To get the mark for **T1(iii)** you must do several searches on your database to prove that it works. You must include validation routines to prove you have thoroughly tested your database. You must also use different standard letters to test that aspect. You must write about each test. You must add each test to your test plan and write down the expected results. For each test you must get a printout to show the results. For example you would include a printout of a validation check working

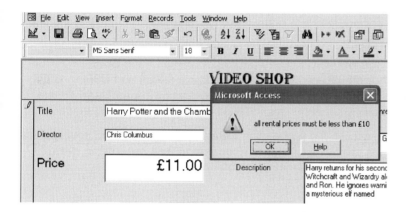

In order to get the mark for **T1(iv)** you must get somebody else to test your solution. The best person for this is the actual video shop manager. If that is not possible you must get somebody to act the role of the video shop manager. Unfortunately, this means that it must be an adult (not a class mate) who knows something about video shops and how they work.

The comments you get from this person must be critical otherwise you may not be awarded the mark. You would do well to produce a response sheet, on which the person can put their comments down. On your response sheet you should include questions about each aspect of your solution and how easy it was for the person to use. You should include questions about whether or not the different aspects of the solution did actually work as intended. It must mention some things which don't work properly or some things which should be in the system but aren't.

To get the mark for **T2(ii)** you must compare the actual results with the expected results for **every** test. It may be that there is not very much to say as the actual results will be identical to the expected results. However this will not always be the case because you typed in the wrong search conditions or you have typed in incorrect data or the wrong variable names were used in a mail merged letter.

Many students fail to get **T2(iii)** because they don't understand the meaning of test data. The test data is the actual data you have typed into your database. It is not the data typed in a query. For example, if you are looking for the customer number 12345, the test data is not the 12345 you type into the query criteria:

The test data is all the data you chose to type into the database. It would include a customer number which is equal to 12345 but also several which are not. Hopefully only one record would be printed out if your solution worked properly. Another example would be to prove that a range check on price worked as it should. When you entered all your test data into the database, you would hopefully have typed in some normal data (data inside the range which would be accepted by the validation check), some abnormal data (data too big or too small so that an error message is produced) and some extreme data which is exactly equal to lowest amount allowed for a price or the largest price allowed (if an error message is produced this means that you have not chosen the limits of the range carefully enough).

User documentation

In your **User documentation** section you must now write down a list of instructions which will help somebody to use your solution. It is not a guide to using the software. It is a guide to show somebody how to use the system you have implemented.

Here is a list of tasks which you will need to carry out to get marks for the **User documentation** section. They are labelled **U1(i)**, **U1(ii)**, **U2(i)** to **U2(iii)** and **U3(i)** to **U3(ii)**. Use the subheadings below and put your work for each subheading in your **User documentation** section.

For tasks **U1(i)** and **U1(ii)** you will use the subheading **Entering, amending and saving data**. For **U2(i)** to **U2(iii)** you will just use the subheading **Processing and outputting data**. For **U3(i)** and **U3(ii)** you will use the subheading **Troubleshooting guide**

TASK U1(i): Produce a user guide which will allow somebody reading it to enter and save data. Put this part of the User Guide under the heading **Entering, amending and saving data**. Again, don't be tempted to copy down word for word what follows as there are missing steps. In this guide you will tell them how to:

- load your database, e.g. *First of all you have to click on …*
- choose the Forms option, e.g. *The next thing to do is to …*
- move to the end of the records and type in a new record, e.g. *You click on the arrow at …*
- save the data, e.g. *Click on the close icon …*

If you do task U1(i) successfully you will get 1 mark.

TASK U1(ii): Produce a user guide which is detailed enough for a competent computer user to add new records. It will also show them how to change data and then save the work. You must write about the database and the word processor and how to do all three things for both types of software. You must include screenshots to make your user guide easy to follow. This will go under the heading **Entering, amending and saving data**.

You should include a screenshot for every step you are writing about.

For example, taking the third step in U1(i):

- How to move to the end of the records and type in a new record, e.g. *You click on the arrow at ...*

If you do task U1(ii) successfully you will get 2 marks.

VIDEO SHOP

Title	Harry Potter and the Chamber of Secrets
Director	Chris Columbus
Price	£4.00
Certificate	PG
Playing time	161
Video Number	1

Actors	Danie
Description	Harry Witch and F a mys
Customer Number	10001
Date borrowed	02/0
Number of days borrowed for	

Record: |◄ ◄ | 2 ► ►| ►*| of 2 ◄|

TASK U2(I): Produce a user guide which will allow somebody reading it to carry out a search on your database. Put this under the heading **Processing and outputting data**. Again, don't be tempted to copy down, word for word what follows as there are missing steps. In this guide you will tell them how to:

- load your database, e.g. *First of all you have to click on ...*
- choose the queries option, e.g. *The next thing to do is to ...*
- select the fields, e.g. *You click on the field you want, then you ...*
- type in the criteria, e.g. *in the row labelled Criteria ...*
- print out the results, e.g. *Click on file ...*

If you do task U2(i) successfully you will get 1 mark.

TASK U2(II): Produce a user guide which is detailed enough for a competent computer user to create a query and print out the results. It will also show a user how to create a standard letter and print it out. You must include screen dumps to make your user guide easy to follow. Put this under the heading **Processing and outputting data**.

You should include a screenshot for every step you are writing about.

For example, in step 4 in U2(i):

- How to type in the criteria, e.g. *in the row labelled Criteria ...*

If you do task U2(ii) successfully you will get 2 marks.

Field:	Surname	First names	Customer Number
Table:	customers	customers	customers
Sort:			
Show:	☑	☑	☑
Criteria:			
or:			

TASK U2(III): Produce a user guide which is detailed enough for a competent computer user to create different types of query for the videos and the customer database and print out the results. It will also show a user how to create different standard letters and print them out. You must include screenshots to make your user guide easy to follow. It will also show users how to use different types of output format. This will go under the heading **Processing and outputting data**. You should include a screenshot for every step you are writing about.

If you do tasks U2(ii) and U2(iii) successfully you will get 3 marks.

TASK U3(I): Under the heading **Troubleshooting guide** you will write down some useful advice to users so that they can avoid potential problems. You must write down **at least two** problems that can happen when the user uses the system. These are not hardware or software problems like what to do when the printer is out of paper. They are meant to be problems that a user might have with your database or standard letter.

For example, one error you could write about is what happens if someone were to type in the wrong search conditions. They will need to be careful when typing in the search conditions. If they misspell the name of a customer or video they will get the wrong output. You should provide examples of what happens when the wrong data is typed in with a screenshot. The two problems must not be similar in nature. This means that you should not give two examples of typing in wrong search criteria.

If you do task U3(i) successfully you will get 1 mark.

TASK U3(II): In addition to what you wrote for task U3(ii) you must write about how these problems can be avoided. One of the simplest methods is verification. Before carrying out a query the user should be told to write down the query they want to type in. They should then read through what they have typed in. They should then compare it to what they have written down. You must do this for the two problems you highlighted in U3(i).

If you do tasks U3(i) and U3(ii) successfully you will get 2 marks.

Evaluation

The last section consists of four tasks, E1–E4. Write these under the heading **Evaluation**.

TASK E1: Write down some simple statements about what your solution can do, such as:

- the Videos database contains information about videos and allows you to search for information about all the videos directed by a particular director;
- you can also get a list of overdue videos;
- the Customer database contains data about the customers and allows you to search for information about where the customer lives if you need to send them a letter.

Make a list of all the things your solution can do.

If you do task E1 successfully you will get 1 mark.

TASK E2:   Now you must write down how you have tackled all the problems you wrote about in your **Analysis** section.

The best way of doing this is to write down all the problems, one by one and then write down after each problem how well you think your database and standard letter works.

Write down each user's requirements which you wrote about in your **Analysis** section. After each one write about how well you think your solution meets each requirement.

For example, one of the user's requirements might have been to have printouts of all the overdue videos. You will write this down and say that your testing shows that this has been achieved. You will need to point out where this test is written about e.g. 'the test on page 24 shows this'.

If you do tasks E1 and E2 successfully you will get 2 marks.

TASK E3:   Now you must write about each part of your design and compare each one with the solution you have produced. You will write about:

- the fields you wanted to have;
- the field types you designed;
- the field lengths you chose;
- the validation checks you felt were needed;
- the forms you designed;
- the reports you designed.

After each item you will write about how well you think you have done in creating it. Make sure you are honest and write about parts of your solution which do not work as well as you'd like or perhaps you didn't even manage to get them to work at all.

You must also write about how you could improve your solution so that any problems could be overcome. For example, the Videos database and Customer database have some identical fields. You could save time entering data by linking them in a relational database.

If you do tasks E1, E2 and E3 successfully you will get 3 marks.

TASK E4:   You must now write about how you asked a user of the system for their comments on how good a system it is. Again, it would be better if it were the manager but it could be an adult who has experience of video rentals. You must write about any improvements which could be made to your solution bearing in mind their comments.

A user might feel that only having one field for videos rented by a customer might prove confusing. It might be better to have additional fields for each borrowed video up to the limit a borrower is allowed. You would have to write a little more than this, even to the extent of naming the fields and suggesting how many extra fields would be required.

An example project

Here is a project which achieved a mark of 51

Here is a list of the criteria and where they were met in the project.

		Page numbers where evidence can be found	Maximum Mark	Mark
Analysis 12	Identify a problem	Page 1	4	3
	Use methods of collecting Information	Pages 2, 3	4	4
	Identify the inputs, outputs and processing required	Pages 3, 4 and 5	4	4
Design 12	Produce designs for the data structure	Pages 5, 6 No choice documented.	3	2
	Produce designs for the user Interface	Pages 6, 7 No choice documented.	3	2
	Produce a design for the output formats	Page 7 No choice documented.	3	2
	Produce software and hardware requirements	Page 4 Although the design section does not contain this section, credit has been given for what is written in the Analysis section. Not sufficient detail for "describe".	3	1
Implementation 14	Implement their data structure	Pages 8–10 Changes made and justified.	4	4
	Implement their input and output formats	Pages 11–16 Changes made and justified.	4	4
	Use features of software appropriately	Pages 8–16	4	4
	Combine software features	No evidence. Graphic "cut & paste" not acceptable.	2	0
Testing 7	Describe their testing	Pages 16–18 "Point of view of user" not covered sufficiently to award all marks.	4	3
	Describe the results	Pages 16–18	3	3
User Documentation 7	Show a potential user how to enter, amend and save data.	Pages 18, 19 Saving is by default, but accepted.	2	2
	Show a potential user how to process and output data	Pages 19, 21	3	3
	Show a potential user how to avoid problems	Page 21	2	2
Evaluation 4	Evaluate their solution	Page 22 Too little comment about user requirements for 4 marks.	4	3

Subtotal (56)	46
Communication (4)	4
Total (60)	50

Car Company

Introduction

Netherfield Motors is a company which sells new and second-hand cars. I visited the company and gave the salesmen questionnaires. When I looked at how they had filled them in I soon began to see the problem they had with their record keeping.

They use a number of filing cabinets to keep all their records about the cars they sell and who they sell them to. There are filing cabinets where they keep the details of each car that they have in stock. Each car's details are kept in a separate folder. There are also filing cabinets for the records of all their customers and the information about each customer is kept in a separate folder. They need the car records so that if a customer comes in and asks for a particular type of car they can look through their folders and see what they have got in stock. They need the customer records so that if they have a delivery of new cars they can read through the customer records and see which customers already have that type of car. They can then send them letters advertising the new cars and inviting them in for a test drive. They also use them for when a customer phones in about a problem with a car – they can look up their details to see how long they've had the car.

Analysis

The Problem

1 When a customer comes in and asks about a certain make of car the salesmen find it difficult to give answers quickly.

   At the moment all the information about each car is written on paper in a separate folder. Each piece of paper has the details of the car including make, model, colour, size of engine, miles on the clock, price, and year of manufacture. When a customer comes in and asks about a certain car the salesmen have to look through these folders to see if it is in stock or not.

2 When a customer comes in and asks about cars in a certain price range the salesmen usually have to forget all about the folders and go outside and look for cars in that price range. The same is true for particular engine sizes, colours and so on.

3 The receptionist is given the job every Monday morning of searching through the customer records to find customers who've had a car for 11 months. They can then send them a letter telling them that it is time for an MOT. She finds it hard to search through all the records. Although she has a standard letter to send them she has to fill in the missing details (like name and address) by hand.

4 When new cars come in the salesmen have to start a new folder for each car. They also have to look through all the customer records and see which ones already own cars of that type. This takes a long time. When they find them they have to send a letter to offer a test drive. This is just a standard flier with no personal details. It would be better if they could take the time to make it more personal.

■ Collecting information

I used questionnaires to collect my information. First of all I decided to ask the following questions:

1 What details about your cars and your customers do you keep and how do you keep them?

2 Can you give me four examples of the types of thing that a customer asks for when they come in looking for a car?

3 When you get a delivery of new cars what sorts of things do you have to do using your records?

4 Are there any jobs that you have to do regularly using your records?

5 How do you keep in touch with your customers?

I needed to know how they kept the information about all their cars and customers. I wanted to keep it short so that they wouldn't feel as though filling in the questionnaire would be a hard thing to do.

I asked these questions because I thought they would give me the most information about all the details of cars and customers that were kept. It would tell me the sort of processing that might go on. It would also tell me what outputs there would be. Questions 1, 4 and 5 would help me work out what type of software I might need. Question 2 would help me decide the processing required for the car records. Question 3 would help me to know what sort of updating would need to go on.

I could have gone down to interview the salesmen but I soon realized on my first visit that this would be a very difficult task. I only just about had time to ask the manager if it would be alright to do my project on them and if I could give them questionnaires to fill in. They seemed so busy. The salesmen in the office always seemed to be talking to customers. There were some who weren't in the office. They were out doing test drives with customers.

The advantages of an interview is that you get honest answers and that you can change your questions depending on the answers you are getting. You can also think up some new questions if you suddenly notice something. You can't do either of these two things if you have already given them a questionnaire. The big disadvantage of interviewing is that it can take a long time. If you had to spend 20 minutes with six salesmen that is two hours! It would also be very unlikely that the manager would allow you to talk to a salesman for 20 minutes when he could be selling a car. This would not be a problem with questionnaires as you could just leave them with the salesmen and they could fill them in when they had time to spare.

I could have gone down and watched the salesmen in action but I think I would have got in the way. Also, customers give the salesmen personal details and I don't think they would like me overhearing. When the salesmen needed to go outside looking at cars I don't think they would like me getting in the way. When they were looking for folders I would have to keep asking to look at documents and that would slow them down. All in all I think that questionnaires are the best way.

Here is part of an example of a returned questionnaire:

Netherfield Motors Questionnaire

1 What details about your cars and your customers do you keep and how do you keep them?

The car details are Make, model, colour, size of engine, miles on the clock, price, year of manufacture. We keep the details of each car in a separate folder...

2 Can you give me four examples of the types of thing that a customer asks for when they come in looking for a car?

1 I can only spend £5000 on a car. What have you got for that price?
2 I want a Ford Focus less than 5 years old.
3 I want a Ford but it must be blue!
4 I want an economical car, say engine size less than 1.4 litres.

3 When you get a delivery of new cars what sorts of things do you have to do using your records?

First we have to get a new form to fill out showing the make and model etc.

Next we have ...

4 Are there any jobs that you have to do regularly using your records?

Every Monday morning as soon as she gets in the receptionist has to look through all the customer records ...

5. How do you keep in touch with your customers?

We don't really, apart from the MOT or new deliveries. Mind you, they keep in touch with us ...

■ Inputs, Outputs, Processing

If we look at the four customer questions listed in the response to question 2 of my questionnaire, we can see what the inputs and outputs are:

■■ INPUTS

In 1 the input is the price.

In 2 the input is the make, model and year of manufacture.

In 3 the input is the make and colour.

In 4 the input is the size of engine.

■■ OUTPUTS

In 1 the output would probably be the make, model, year of manufacture and the price.

In 2 the output would probably be the make, model, year of manufacture and price.

In 3 the output would probably be the make, colour, model and price.

In 4 the output would probably be the make, model, size of engine and price.

■■ PROCESSING

In 1 the salesman looks at the folders for all the cars costing less than £5000. He copies down make, model, year of manufacture and the price, then shows the customer this list.

In 2 the salesman will look through the folders. He looks for all the Ford cars and any folders he finds he puts in a separate pile. He now looks through all these and sorts out the ones that are Focuses. Finally with this fresh pile he looks to see which are less than 5 years old and he writes down the make, model, year of manufacture and price.

In 3 the salesman will look through the folders. He looks for all the Ford cars and any folders he finds he puts in a pile. He now looks through all these and writes down all the ones that are blue. He writes down their make, colour, model and price.

In 4 the salesman will look through the folders for all the cars whose engine size is less than 1.4 litres. He writes down the make, model, size of engine and price of them.

■■ OTHER INPUTS, PROCESSING AND OUTPUTS

MOTs

Input: this is the date the car was bought. This is so the receptionist can find all the cars bought about 11 months ago.

Processing: the receptionist prints out a number of standard MOT letters. She looks through all the customer records for all the dates of purchase which are about 11 months ago. She will write in the name and address of the customer on the letter.

Output: name, address and date of purchase.

New cars

Input: the make and model of the new car and the date of purchase of current car.

Processing: the salesmen look through all the customer records and see which ones already own cars of that make and model. They then look through these to find which customers have had their current cars for more than a year. They write down their names and addresses for the envelopes which will contain the standard flier.

Output: the names and addresses of the customers.

■ System Specification

■■ SOFTWARE

It is quite clear to see that the showroom needs a database which will hold all the records of the customers and the stock. The customer file will store details about the customers and the cars they own. The stock file will be about the cars in the showroom which have yet to be sold and not about the cars that have already been sold. This means that the software doesn't need to be able to produce a relational database. The software must also be able to produce standard letters. A word processor which can get the information from a database and put it into a standard letter would be best.

■■ HARDWARE

One system might be:

- A desktop computer with 40GB hard disk
- DVD/CD rewriter
- 4 GB processor
- top quality graphics card with TV out
- 17 inch monitor

■■■ ALTERNATIVE SYSTEM

They could go for a cheaper, slower processor and a system with less graphics capability as well as a smaller monitor. I think this would be better as they would only need a top-range graphics card if they used it for playing complex games and the same for a large monitor. They are only going to need it for searching databases and producing standard letters and so could settle for a smaller cheaper system.

They could go for a spreadsheet package with separate worksheets for cars and customers. It could be used with a word processor to create mail-merged letters. The advantage is that it could be used to do calculations on prices and profit margins. There are many disadvantages though. It would be harder to search for certain cars or customers. Mail-merging is a lot harder. I think it would be better to have a database and a word processor which are easy to use together like Microsoft Office or Works.

■ Design

■ Data structure

Field name	Field type	Field length	Validation Check
Make	Text	20	None
Model	Text	20	None
Year made	Number	9999	<2006
Price	Currency	£99999	<100000
Colour	Text	15	None
Size of engine	Number/Integer	9.9	<10.0

Here was my first attempt at designing a database structure. I used all the fields I wrote about in my Inputs, outputs, processing section:

Next I wanted to make sure that I had all the right fields – I'd got the right structure. I collected some information about cars and copied them on to a data capture form which is on the next page.

As you can see, I had to add some more fields. As well as the ones I had got already I saw that lots of adverts had information about: mileage; number of doors; if it had air-conditioning; if it had airbags;

Colour	Make	Model	Price	Year made	Mileage	Number of doors	Engine size	Air conditioning	Air bags
Silver	Peugeot	307	£5,995	2001	27,000	3	1.4	No	Twin
Silver	Peugeot	406	£3,200	1996	28,000	4	2.0	No	No
Burgundy	Renault	Clio	£2,745	1998	59,000	3	1.2	No	No
Red	Renault	Clio	£1,295	1998	45,000	3	1.2	No	No
Green	Renault	Clio	£3,895	2000	20,000	3	1.2	No	Twin
Red	Citroen	Saxo	£2,779	1999	31,765	3	1.0	No	No
Silver	Vauxhall	Astra	£3,025	1998	51,089	5	1.6	Yes	Drivers
Red	Peugeot	106	£3,299	1999	49,206	3	1.1	No	No
Blue	Renault	Laguna	£3,495	1998	52,469	5	1.8	Yes	Twin
Red	Toyota	Avensis	£3,495	1998	51,894	5	1.8	No	No
Blue	Ford	Fiesta	£3,528	1998	40,171	3	1.2	No	Drivers
Silver	Toyota	Corolla	£3,795	1998	63,011	5	1.3	No	No
Gold	Rover	25	£4,199	2000	55,891	3	1.6	No	Drivers
Red	Fiat	Punto	£4,199	2001	21,255	3	1.2	No	Twin
Blue	Citroen	Xsara	£4,699	1998	44,369	5	1.9	Yes	Twin
Silver	Mazda	Premacy	£5,199	1999	65,370	5	1.8	Yes	Drivers
Silver	Nissan	Almera	£5,399	2001	12,416	3	1.5	No	Drivers
Red	Toyota	Yaris	£5,639	2002	10,363	5	1.0	No	Drivers
Blue	Peugeot	406	£5,745	1999	26,000	4	1.8	Yes	Twin
Black	Smart	City	£6,000	2002	4,975	2	0.7	No	Twin
Green	Vauxhall	Corsa	£6,499	2003	13,234	5	1.2	No	Drivers
Grey	Vauxhall	Vectra	£6,695	2000	51,242	5	1.8	Yes	Twin
Silver	Ford	Focus	£6,750	2001	21,488	5	1.6	Yes	Twin
Blue	Honda	Accord	£6,995	1998	77,250	2	3.0	No	No
Silver	Rover	45	£6,995	2001	53,997	4	2.0	Yes	Drivers

I had to change some of the field types and lengths. For each field I looked at the data I had collected on my data capture form. I saw that I had got my original structure right except for field lengths and field type for engine size. I had to change the field type from integer to decimal because most adverts had a decimal number like 1.4 instead of 1400. Air conditioning has the answers yes or no so I chose text. Air bags only had three answers, no, twin and drivers, so I chose text.

When I looked at the data I saw that most of my fields didn't need to be so long. What I did now was I looked for the longest piece of data in each field and added 2 characters just in case I needed spaces between columns in my output. The longest make is Volkswagen which is 10 characters long so I made it 12. The longest colour is Burgundy which is 8 so I made it 10. The longest model is Avensis with 7 so I made it 9. The longest answer to air conditioning is yes so I made that 5. The longest piece of data in Air bags was drivers (7) so I made it 9.

Field name	Field type	Field length	Validation Check	Example
Make	Text	12	None	Volkswagen
Model	Text	9	None	Premacy
Year made	Number	9999	<2006	2001
Price	Currency	£99999	<100000	£32,000
Colour	Text	10	None	Burgundy
Size of engine	Decimal	9.9	<10.0	1.8
Mileage	Number/Integer	99999	<100000	21253
Number of doors	Number/Integer	9	<6	5
Air conditioning	Text	5	None	Yes
Airbags	Text	9	None	Drivers

The advantage of the first design is that there are fewer fields which will save time for the person typing in the data. It also matches the user's needs since the fields used come from the questions he suggested. The disadvantages are that customers might come in and ask for cars with features that aren't included in this design. Another disadvantage is that it would waste space on the hard drive as the fields will have more spaces than they need.

The advantages of the second design are that the fields used are like the ones which other car showrooms would use so they wouldn't lose business for not being able to answer customer questions. A disadvantage is that there is a lot more data for the typist to type in and this could lead to more mistakes.

■ User interface

I now had to design the computer screen I would use to type in my data. Here was what I thought of at first:

Make ▭	Model ▭
Year made ▭	Price ▭
Colour ▭	Size of engine ▭
Mileage ▭	Number of doors ▭
Air conditioning ▭	Airbags ▭

Looking at it I thought that one or two improvements were needed. The first would be the moving of Mileage underneath Make. I think that Mileage and Price are the two most important fields after Make and Model. These could be made bigger to show their importance.

The advantage of the first design is that it is small and compact and allows the person typing in the data to do it without being distracted by different size fields etc. The disadvantage is that the typist would be switching between text and numeric fields a lot of the time. It might be easier if all the text fields were at the top followed by the numeric data. These last fields could be entered quickly because you would only need to use the number pad. The advantage of the second design is that the more important fields are highlighted in a bigger font which will make the typist concentrate. The disadvantage is that the typist should really be concentrating on all the fields not just making sure some are right.

Make		Model	
Mileage		Price	
Colour		Size of engine	
Year made		Number of doors	
Air conditioning		Airbags	

■ Output formats

For my output formats I am going to concentrate on the printed reports which the system will produce. I know that most outputs on the system will be to the monitor but printed reports will be needed. These are very important because they will be taken away by the customers and other people will see them. If they don't look very professional then this could lose sales. Here was my first idea (right):

Cars with air conditioning and twin air bags

Make: Renault
Model: Laguna
Price: £3496
Year made: 1998
Mileage: 52489
Number of doors: 5
Engine size: 1.8
Air conditioning: ✓
Airbags: twin

Here is my second idea:

Netherfield Autos

Cars with air conditioning and twin air bags

Make	Model	Price	Year	Mileage	Number of doors	Engine size	Air conditioning	Airbags
Renault	Laguna	£3495	1998	52489	5	1.8	✓	twin
Peugeot	406	£5795	1999	26000	4	1.8	✓	twin

The advantage of the first design is for the customer you could print out one sheet for each car. The disadvantage for the owner is that it would waste a lot of paper. It would be easier to lose one of the records. The advantage with the second one is that you could arrange to have the name of the company on every sheet and a picture of a car which makes it look more professional. The disadvantage is that in order to get the column headings to fit in the data is not spread out evenly.

■ Implementation

■■ **Implementing the data structure**

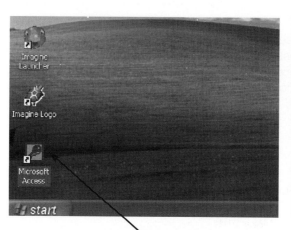

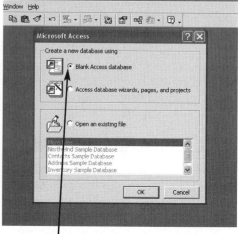

This is how I created my database. First of all I loaded up Microsoft Access by clicking on the Access icon on the desktop.

When I got this screen up I clicked on Blank database.

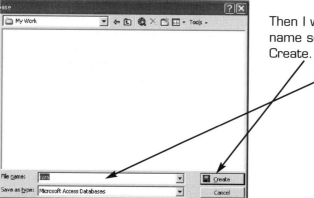

Then I was asked to give the database a name so I typed in 'cars' and clicked on Create.

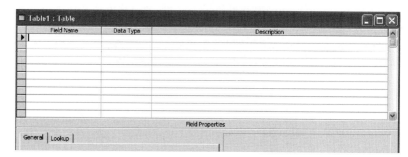

Then the design screen came up:

I typed in the first field name which was Make and pressed TAB which took me to field

Field Name	Data Type	Description
Make	Text	Company making car, field size 12

Field Properties

General | Lookup

Field Size	12
Format	
Input Mask	

type which I left as Text. I pressed TAB again. I typed in the Description. I clicked on Field Size and I changed the field length to 12.

I then typed in all the field names, field types and descriptions.

stock : Table

Field Name	Data Type	Description
Make	Text	Company making car. field size 12
Model	Text	Model name of car. field size 8
Year made	Number	The year the car was made. 4 digit number
Price	Currency	Price the car is being sold for. 4 digit number with £
Colour	Text	Colour of car. field size 10
Engine size	Number	The size of the car engine in litres. A two figure nu
Mileage	Number	Number of miles the car has gone since it was made
Number of doors	Number	Number of doors the car has got. A one digit numbe
Air conditioning	Yes/No	To see if the car has air conditioning. yes or no
Air bags	Text	to see if the car has driver air bag, driver and pass

Field Properties

General | Lookup

Field Size	Decimal
Format	
Precision	2
Scale	1
Decimal Places	1
Input Mask	
Caption	
Default Value	0
Validation Rule	<10
Validation Text	you must type in a size less than 10
Required	No
Indexed	No

The data type deter
store in the field

When I changed a field type to number I then had to choose the type of number from a drop down list. If I changed it to decimal I had to tell the computer how many digits I wanted it to (precision) and how many figures after the decimal place I wanted (scale and decimal places).

I also typed in that the number should always be less than 10 (<10) for the validation rule. For the validation text I typed in the message I wanted to come on the screen if someone typed in a number 10 or bigger.

When I was creating my structure I saw that you could have yes/no fields. I immediately changed the field type for Air conditioning from text to yes/no as this was going to make it easier to click on it instead of typing in yes or no all the time.

When I started to type in the data it was annoying to have to keep typing in drivers or twin or none for Airbags. I found out that you could use a lookup field and this is how I changed it from text to lookup:

I clicked on the drop down list next to text (like I had when I changed other fields from text to number or yes/no) and clicked on Lookup wizard.

Then this box came up so I clicked on this and then clicked on Next.

I typed the three different values in and clicked on Next.

This box came up and I was happy for it to be called Air bags so I clicked on Finish. Now when I needed to type in the type of airbags I just had to click on an item from the list.

Implementing the input and output formats

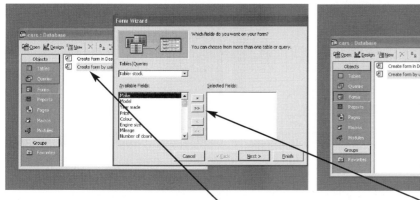

From the main screen I clicked on Create forms using wizard and this came up:

I clicked on the double arrow to choose all the fields and clicked on Next. On the next screen I clicked on Columnar and then Next.

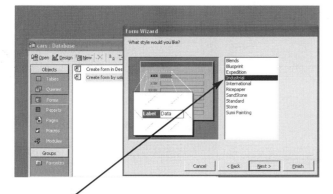

On this screen I chose Industrial.

I called it stock and clicked on Modify form design and clicked on Finish.

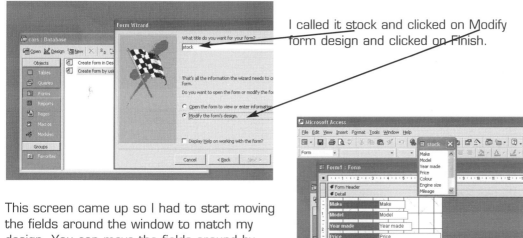

This screen came up so I had to start moving the fields around the window to match my design. You can move the fields around by dragging them with the mouse. You can make them bigger by dragging the corners and stretching them out.

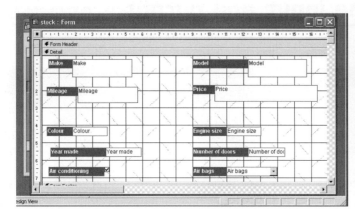 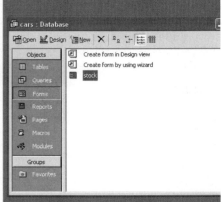

This is what I ended up with:

When I clicked on the cross it asked me if I wanted to save the work so I said yes.

This came back and I clicked on stock and then I typed in my data. I just clicked in each box and typed it in.

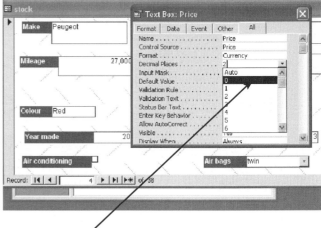

I noticed that although I had made the number of decimal places 0 for price in my structure, it was coming up with two decimal places on the form.

I clicked on the left hand button and clicked on Properties.

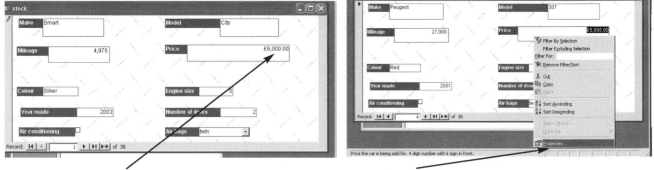

I clicked on decimal places and clicked on the drop down menu and clicked on 0.

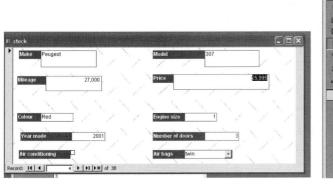

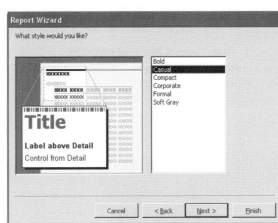

Now it worked.

The next thing I had to do was to create my reports. I clicked on create report using wizard and this came up.

From the drop down list I chose the query 'twin airbags and air conditioning'

I chose my fields by clicking on each one and clicking on the single forward arrow. I didn't use colour. I clicked on Next.

When this window came up I clicked on Tabular and then Next.

I chose Casual and clicked Next.

I typed in a title 'twin airbags and air conditioning'. I clicked on Modify the report design and clicked on Finish.

I clicked on the title box and changed the words to make it look like my design. I clicked on the right hand button of the mouse because the font was wrong

I scrolled down and got this:

I changed it to Comic Sans MS size 14 so it fitted on one line.

Next I widened the Report header space. In the top I drew a new box and typed in Netherfield Motors. I right- clicked the box. I scrolled down until I could see the font name and size. I changed it to Franklin Gothic Book snd size 18.

I then copied and pasted the picture of the car that I had found on the Internet.

Here it is changed in design view

(14)

Here it is when you click on the report.

As you can see the names don't fit in the spaces and some of the headings wouldn't fit the way I had them in the original design.

I had to widen some of the boxes. I also had to widen the Page Header space.

I then had to make Year wider. I also had to change the sizes of boxes and make some of the fields centre-aligned so that everything fitted.

Boxes made bigger.

Centred.

When I clicked on the report it
now fitted like this:

Netherfield Motors

Cars with twin air bags and air conditioning

Make	Model	Price	Year made	Mileage	Number of doors	Engine size	Air cond	Air bags
Renault	Laguna	£3,495	1998	52,469	5	1.8	☑	twin
Peogeot	406	£5,795	1999	26,000	4	1.8	☑	twin
Vauxhall	Vectra	£6,895	2000	51,242	5	1.8	☑	twin
Ford	Focus	£6,750	2001	21,488	5	1.6	☑	twin
Renault	Migane	£7,595	2000	26,556	5	1.6	☑	twin
Nissan	Almera	£8,299	2001	24,385	5	1.8	☑	twin

■ My finished database

Make	Model	Year made	Price	Colour	Engine size	Mileage	Number of doors	Air conditioning	Air bags
Peugeot	406	1996	£3,200	Silver	1.8	28,000	4	☐	none
Peugeot	406	1999	£5,795	Silver	1.8	26,000	4	☑	twin
Volkswagen	Bora	2003	£9,999	Red	1.6	13,700	4	☑	drivers
Vauxhall	Astra	1998	£3,025	Blue	1.8	51,894	5	☑	drivers
Renault	Laguna	1998	£3,495	Black	1.8	52,469	5	☑	twin
Toyota	Avensis	1998	£3,495	Green	1.8	51,894	5	☐	none
Toyota	Corolla	1998	£3,795	Green	1.3	63,011	5	☐	none
Citroen	Xantia	1998	£4,699	Silver	1.9	44,369	5	☑	drivers
Mazda	Premacy	1999	£5,199	Blue	1.8	65,370	5	☑	drivers
Vauxhall	Corsa	2003	£6,499	Silver	1.2	13,234	5	☐	drivers
Vauxhall	Vectra	2000	£6,695	Green	1.8	51,242	5	☑	twin
Ford	Focus	2001	£6,750	Silver	1.6	21,488	5	☑	twin
Rover	45	2001	£6,995	Red	2	53,997	5	☑	drivers
Volkswagen	Golf	1998	£7,000	Silver	1.6	56,007	5	☐	twin
Ford	Fiesta	2003	£7,186	Red	1.4	6,883	5	☑	drivers
Ford	Focus	2000	£7,199	Silver	2	46,347	5	☑	drivers
Toyota	Picnic	1998	£7,295	Red	2	61,113	5	☐	none
Renault	Migane	2000	£7,595	Silver	1.6	26,556	5	☑	twin
Volvo	V40	1999	£7,999	Silver	2	61,150	5	☐	none
Nissan	Almera	2001	£8,299	Blue	1.8	24,385	5	☑	twin
Toyota	Avensis	2002	£9,199	Gold	2	21,002	5	☑	twin
Honda	CR-V	1999	£9,499	Silver	2	60,315	5	☑	twin
Ford	Mondeo	2003	£9,999	Black	1.8	13,505	5	☑	drivers

Here is the printout of my complete database:

■ Testing

Having entered all my data I now had to test that the database worked. Here was my
test plan together with the actual results. I will use the customer questions I put in my
Analysis section:

1 I can only spend £5000 on a car. What have you got for that price?
2 I want a Ford Focus less than 5 years old.

Test	Expected results	Actual results	Comment
Price <= 5000	A list of cars £5000 or less	A list of cars £5000 or less	As expected
Make = Ford Model = Focus Year made > 2000	A list of all the Ford Focus's made after 2000	A list of all the Ford Focus's made after 2000	As expected
Make = Ford Colour = blue	A list of all the blue Fords	A list of all the blue Fords	As expected
Engine size <1.4	A list of all the cars less than 1.4 litres	A list of all the cars less than 1.4 litres	As expected
type in 2006 in Year made field	error message saying year is too big	error message saying year is too big	As expected
type in 120000 in Price field	error message saying price is too big	error message saying price is too big	As expected
type in 11 in engine size field	error message saying engine size is too big	error message saying engine size is too big	As expected
type in 111000 in mileage field	error message saying mileage is too big	error message saying mileage is too big	As expected
type in 6 in number of doors	error message saying number is too big	error message saying number is too big	As expected

3 I want a Ford but it must be blue!

4 I want an economical car, say engine size less than 1.4 litres

And I will test my validation routines.

Here is the design of the first query

Here are the results

Here is the design for my number of doors validation check.

Make	Model	Year made	Price
Peugeot	406	1996	£3,200
Renault	Clio	1998	£2,795
Renault	Clio	1998	£1,295
Renault	Clio	2000	£3,895
Citroen	Saxo	1999	£2,779
Vauxhall	Astra	1998	£3,025
Peugeot	106	1999	£3,299
Renault	Laguna	1998	£3,495
Toyota	Avenses	1998	£3,495
Ford	Fiesta	1998	£3,528
Toyota	Corolla	1998	£3,795
Rover	25	2000	£4,199
Fiat	Punto	2001	£4,199
Citroen	Xantia	1998	£4,699
			£0

Field Name	Data Type	Description
Make	Text	Company making car. field size 12
Model	Text	Model name of car. field size 8
Year made	Number	The year the car was made. 4 digit number
Price	Currency	Price the car is being sold for. 4 digit number with £ sign in front
Colour	Text	Colour of car. field size 10
Engine size	Number	The size of the car engine in litres. A two figure number to 1 dec
Mileage	Number	Number of miles the car has gone since it was made. 5 digit num
Number of doors	Number	Number of doors the car has got. A one digit number.
Air conditioning	Yes/No	To see if the car has air conditioning. yes or no
Air bags	Text	to see if the car has driver air bag, driver and passenger airbags

Field Properties

General | Lookup

Field Size	Long Integer
Format	
Decimal Places	Auto
Input Mask	
Caption	
Default Value	0
Validation Rule	>1 And <6
Validation Text	Number of doors must be between 2 and
Required	No
Indexed	Yes (Duplicates OK)

The data type determines the kind the field. Press F1 fo

Here is proof it works.

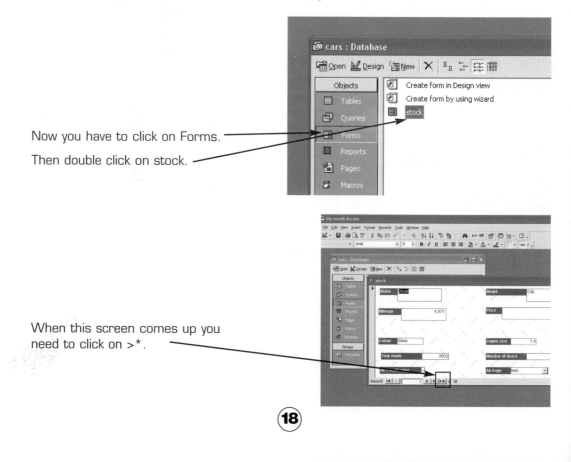

I chose test data that would test the queries. I also chose data which met the criteria but I made sure there was plenty of data that did not. For example, I used Ford for some makes, Focus for some models and 2001 for year. I also had cars which were not Fords, Fords which were not Focuses and a Ford Focus which was older than 2001.

For validation checks I made sure that there were numbers at extreme ends of a range. For example, I had 2 and 5 for the number of doors as well as trying to type in abnormal data such as 6.

■ User documentation

■ How to enter data

Follow the instructions on page 16. Do not click on blank Access database but click on open an existing file. Click on Cars and click on Open.

Now you have to click on Forms.

Then double click on stock.

When this screen comes up you need to click on >*.

This takes you to the end of the database and the next blank record. You just click on each box in turn and type in the data. For Air conditioning you just click the box if there is air conditioning and leave it blank if there isn't. If you tick it by mistake just click on it again and the tick will disappear.

To change the data in a record just load the database up and click on Forms and stock as above, but this time click on the little arrow and this will take you to the next record. Keep clicking until you get to the record you want. When you get to it, just click on the box you want to change and delete the data and type in the new data.

To save your database, you don't have to do anything with Access; you just close the database down (click on the cross) and it automatically saves.

■ How to do a search

After you have loaded up the database you click on Create query by using wizard. You get this.

Make sure it says Table:stock here. If it doesn't click on the down arrow and click on Table:stock. Now click on the double arrow and you will get the screen overleaf.

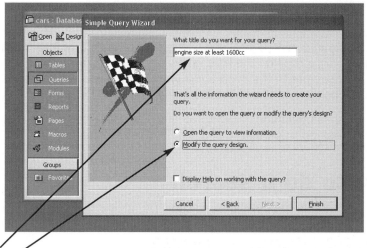

Keep clicking on Next till you get this screen:

Type in the title (this query will find all the engine sizes 1.6 litres and over). Click on Modify query design and click on Next.

This screen comes up and you type in your criteria in the Criteria row:

You type in <=1.6 in the Engine size column. Now all you do is to click on the close icon and you will get this message:

Click on Yes and you get this:

If you now double-click on the query you should get these results:

Make	Model	Year made	Price	Colour	Engine size	Mileage	Number of doors	Air
Toyota	Avenses	1998	£3,495	Green	1.8	51,894	5	
Rover	25	2000	£4,199	Blue	1.6	55,891	3	
Citroen	Xantia	1998	£4,699	Silver	1.9	44,369	5	
Mazda	Premacy	1999	£5,199	Blue	1.8	65,370	5	
Peugeot	406	1999	£5,795	Silver	1.8	26,000	4	
Vauxhall	Vectra	2000	£6,695	Green	1.8	51,242	5	
Ford	Focus	2001	£6,750	Silver	1.6	21,488	5	
Honda	Accord	1998	£6,995	Silver	3	77,250	2	
Rover	45	2001	£6,995	Red	2	53,997	5	
Volkswagen	Golf	1998	£7,000	Silver	1.6	56,007	5	
Ford	Focus	2000	£7,199	Silver	2	46,347	5	
Toyota	Picnic	1998	£7,295	Red	2	61,113	5	
Renault	Migane	2000	£7,595	Silver	1.6	26,556	5	
Volvo	V40	1999	£7,999	Silver	2	61,150	5	
Mazda	MX-5	2000	£8,199	Burgundy	1.6	58,904	2	
Nissan	Almera	2001	£8,299	Blue	1.8	24,385	5	
Ford	Focus	2003	£8,995	Blue	1.6	14,404	3	
Toyota	Avensis	2002	£9,199	Gold	2	21,002	5	
Honda	CR-V	1999	£9,499	Silver	2	60,315	5	
Ford	Mondeo	2003	£9,999	Black	1.8	13,505	5	
Volkswagen	Bora	2003	£9,999	Red	1.6	13,700	4	
*			£0		0	0	0	

To print them out, you click on the print icon and these results will print out.

■ Troubleshooting guide

There are a number of errors you can make. When you are searching for cars less than £6000 for example, you have to remember that the customer would probably have asked for a car for £6000 or less. In this case you must type in <= 6000 and not just <6000.

Other possible mistakes are that you must type in exact spellings when you are searching on text fields. For example typing in Ford under the make field will have a number of matches but Frod will not.

If you want to know whether a car has air conditioning you type in yes (which is the computer equivalent for a tick) in the Air conditioning column.

If when you click on the query and there are no matching records check that you have done the following properly:

● Typed in the correct criteria.
● Typed the criteria in the correct column.
● Typed in < (less than) and not > (greater than) or the other way round.
● If you can't remember whether the data is CR-V or CR V or CR/V you should type in CR*. This will look for anything beginning CR no matter what it ends in.

■ Evaluation

In my design section I said that I would create a database with this structure:

Field name	Field type	Field length	Validation Check	Example
Make	Text	12	None	Volkswagen
Model	Text	9	None	Premacy
Year made	Number	9999	<2006	2001
Price	Currency	£99999	<100000	£32,000
Colour	Text	10	None	Burgundy
Size of engine	Decimal	9.9	<10.0	1.8
Mileage	Number/Integer	99999	<100000	21253
Number of doors	Number/Integer	9	<6	5
Air conditioning	Text	5	None	Yes
Airbags	Text	9	None	Drivers

I did this as you can see on pages 16 and 17. I did make some minor changes as you can see on pages 18 and 19. These were improvements, I think, as it:

● makes it easier for anyone typing in data
● makes it faster to type in
● leaves less room for mistakes as you aren't typing in all the words in the last two fields

On page 13 you can see my final design for the user interface

On page 22 you can see it implemented. I made some changes but it looks like my design.

I think my report on page 27 looks just like the one I designed.

Although I think it is a good system it is not what I thought it would be after I had done my Analysis section. I have tested it and it works well as you can see in my testing section.

It doesn't have a customer file. I would need to add another file for sold cars into which I would copy cars from the stock file to the sold file when they are sold. I would have a customer file linked to these cars which would have names, addresses, phone numbers, etc. I would also have a mailmerge system so that letters could be word processed and merged with the customer file to produce standard letters. This could be used when a lot of cars of a particular make come in to the showroom and customers who already have that sort of car could be sent a letter telling them newer ones have come in.

Index